9403300033

D0706837

Yale Studies on White-Collar Crime

■ Sitting in Judgment

The Sentencing of
White-Collar Criminals

Stanton Wheeler
Kenneth Mann
Austin Sarat

Yale University Press
New Haven and London

LIBRARY OF MOUNT ST. MARY'S COLLEGE EMMITSBURG, MARYLAND
WITHDRAWN

Copyright © 1988 by Yale University.
All rights reserved.
This book may not be reproduced, in whole
or in part, including illustrations, in
any form (beyond that copying permitted by
Sections 107 and 108 of the U.S. Copyright
Law and except by reviewers for the public
press), without written permission from the
publishers.

Designed by Sally Harris
and set in Times Roman type by
Rainsford Type, Danbury, Connecticut.
Printed in the United States of America by
The Murray Printing Company, Westford,
Massachusetts.

Library of Congress Cataloging-in-Publication Data

Wheeler, Stanton, 1930-
    Sitting in judgment: the sentencing of white-
  collar criminals / Stanton Wheeler, Kenneth
Mann, Austin Sarat.
    p. cm. — (Yale studies on white-collar crime)
    Includes index.
    ISBN 0-300-03983-2 (alk. paper)
    1. Sentences (Criminal procedure)—United
    States. 2. White-collar crimes—United States.
3. Judicial process—United States. I. Mann,
Kenneth, 1947- . II. Sarat, Austin.
III. Title. IV. Series.
KF9685.W47 1988
345.73′0268—dc19
[347.305268]   88-3196
                      CIP   oclc: 17546744

The paper in this book meets the guidelines for
permanence and durability of the Committee on
Production Guidelines for Book Longevity of the
Council on Library Resources.

10 9 8 7 6 5 4 3 2 1

To Marcia (S.W.)

To Gabriela (K.M.)

To George Kateb (A.S.)

■ Contents

■ Preface

This book describes how federal district court judges think about the sentencing of criminals, particularly white-collar criminals. It presents judicial thought, in the judges' own words. So far as we know, it is the most complete record available of how federal judges justify their decisions. We argue that the judges' views reveal a kind of informal common law of sentencing, widely shared by different judges and rooted in historic principles of Anglo-American criminal jurisprudence. For a variety of reasons, that informal common law of sentencing does not lead to an agreement on actual sentences, and in our concluding chapter we outline some of the reasons for the disjuncture between agreed-upon principles and actual outcomes and describe some of the steps that might be taken to bring the two into closer correspondence.

Like many scholarly works, this one has been germinating for some time. When we have discussed the manuscript with colleagues, three issues have arisen repeatedly, and we would like to address each briefly in this preface.

The first is a question of method, or perhaps more generally of scientific validity. How do we know that what the judges told us is what they really do? Our interviewees were experienced judges who certainly were responding seriously to our questions, but there may still be a gap between their words and their actions. In a forthcoming companion volume based on quantitative research, we have ample evidence that the various factors our judges reported as important in their thinking do indeed correlate with the actual sentences meted out in the federal system. Thus there is a reasonably close correspondence between what the judges in our study say and what a much broader sampling of judges actually do.

But to worry about the connection between words and deeds is to misconstrue the fundamental purpose of our inquiry. This is a study of judicial thought as reflected in judicial talk. The study of judicial thought is important in its own right, for it tells us what standards judges think they are invoking as they go about their important task of sentencing. The record of that thought can also provide a basis for principled discussion, criticism, and reform of sentencing.

A second frequent question raised about our work deals with its relationship to the guidelines movement. The major current sentencing reform is the set of guidelines set forth by the recently established Federal Sentencing Commission. In brief, our study was conceived entirely independently of the guidelines movement and prior to the establishment of the current federal guidelines. Our study documents, if you will, how "pre-guidelines" federal judges have been thinking and reasoning about sentencing.

The guidelines were enacted in a climate of haste and controversy, and the legislation mandating the guidelines requires systematic review and revision. One important role for our study vis-à-vis the guidelines is to act as a kind of benchmark for guidelines revision. If one wants to test the "reasonableness" of a new guideline, one might ask whether it incorporates a principle articulated by judges' sentencing prior to the enactment of the guidelines, and if not, whether there is a good independent justification for it. And if the guidelines rule out factors that current sitting judges have frequently relied upon, one should ask if there are good and principled reasons why these factors are being ruled out. Our own position is that while there is much to recommend a guidelines system, the task of developing both reasonable and comprehensive guidelines is a daunting one, especially given the extraordinary variety of white-collar crimes in the federal system. It is a task that can profit from close study of the views and experiences of federal judges who have faced these problems for years.

The third issue concerns the seeming conflict between our major conclusion that federal district court judges, though operating without appellate review, have developed an informal common law of sentencing, and the fact that the system still produces disparate sentences. What does it *mean* to say that there is a common body of principles if there remains unwanted variation in actual sentences? Our answer is that it is important to identify and localize the sources of disparity. If the sources lie primarily in wildly different and contradictory sets of values that federal judges bring to their work, then we may face a kind of chaos that can be resolved only by adopting a set of rigid guidelines.

But if, as our analysis suggests, the problems lie less in fundamental disagreement over basic principles and more in failure to establish mechanisms for translating those principles into particular sentences, then different and arguably less radical approaches to the problem of disparity might be considered. An alternative would be to allow somewhat more discretion for judges, but in a system where the principles are more clearly articulated. We have tried to lay out the currently practiced version of those principles in this book.

We are under no illusion that the issue is a simple one or that we have a panacea. But we do believe the arguments made here, coupled with the evidence of a commonly shared judicial outlook, provide an alternative approach to the major sentencing problems judges face today.

Judges are a critical and understudied part of the culture of the courthouse. We see in that culture a mirror of some of the larger norms and values through which the society rationalizes its treatment of criminals. But the courthouse does more than mirror. When judges sit in judgment, they give voice to the values that determine the fates of all convicted criminals, thereby shaping broader societal judgments. Whatever the practical utility of our work, to us the most important long-term contribution is to bring judicial values into full view.

We are indebted to many institutions and persons for financial, intellectual, and moral support. This book is part of a larger program of research on white-collar crime, supported by Grant No. 78-N1-AX-0017 from the National Institute of Justice, U.S. Department of Justice. We are also heavily indebted to Yale Law School, the home of the broader project for many years, to Abraham S. Goldstein and Albert J. Reiss, Jr., who served on a steering committee for much of the work, and to Deans Harry H. Wellington and Guido Calabresi. One of us (K.M.) is especially indebted to the Faculty of Law at Tel Aviv University for released time.

Throughout the project we have benefited enormously from Daniel J. Freed, not only from his close and thoughtful reading of the manuscript, but from discussions with many participants in his Yale sentencing workshops, including judges and prosecutors, at both state and federal levels.

We are especially indebted to a group of colleagues who were doing collaborative work on white-collar crime at Yale, including Jack Katz and Susan Shapiro, to those who are associated with a forthcoming companion volume, especially David Weisburd and Nancy Bode, and to two research assistants, David Howarth and Clyde Spillinger. Our work also profited from detailed discussions at two Yale Law School faculty workshops and at the Amherst seminar on legal ideology and legal process.

The manuscript has been read in whole or in part by a number of colleagues: Frank Allen, Tom Dumm, Andrew Von Hirsch, Sheldon Messinger, Ilene Nagel, Norval Morris, U.S. Circuit Judge Jon O. Newman, and Michael Tonry. We have not satisfied all their queries, but the book is better because of their close readings.

Marcia Chambers provided not only a fine editorial eye, but also the kind of prod to completion of projects that some academics seem to require.

Finally, we are indebted to those who got the manuscript ready for delivery to Yale University Press, especially Deborah Jones on the West Coast and Liz Vellali and Lurline Dowell on the East; and to those at the Press who have treated the project with special care, Marian Ash and Lawrence Kenney.

We owe a last debt of thanks to each other, for this has been a genuinely collaborative effort. Without the collaboration, this project would have been a much less enjoyable as well as less valuable learning experience for each of us.

Sitting in Judgment

1

Toward a Common Law of Sentencing

The subject of this book lies at the intersection of two central concerns in criminal justice: the sentencing of offenders and the treatment accorded white-collar criminals. The sentencing of convicted defendants is clearly one of the most pivotal events in the administration of justice. For the convicted offender, it is the sentence that will determine how his next few months and years are spent—whether at liberty or under confinement. And for the rest of society, it is the sentence that gives expression to our sentiments and understandings regarding crime and criminals.

Save for the small minority of cases that go to jury trial, the stage of sentencing is the most visible stage in the criminal justice system. If penalties are perceived to be too harsh, we worry about cruelty and ask for compassion. If they are perceived as too lenient we worry about compassion for the victim and whether a deterrent effect will disappear. And if sentences are perceived as arbitrary and capricious, we worry about the fundamental sense of justice in the society. There is thus an understandable concern with sentencing, for the specific ways in which sentences are meted out, and for the effects of sentencing on both offender and the broader community.

Interest in sentencing has reached new heights in the last decade. An earlier theory of rehabilitation came under attack.[1] Sentencing guideline systems emerged to limit and structure judicial discretion.[2] Sentencing authorities debated the wisdom of sentences based on predictions of future conduct rather than on expressions of deserved

1. Andrew von Hirsch, *Doing Justice: The Choice of Punishments* (New York: Hill and Wang, 1976).
2. For a discussion of an early and influential move toward sentencing guidelines, see U.S. Department of Justice, *The Implementation of the California Determinate Sentencing Law* (Washington, D.C.: National Institute of Justice, 1982).

1

punishment for past conduct,[3] and Congress passed a federal sentencing law that promises to alter our modes of sentencing federal offenders in fundamental ways.[4]

The subject of white-collar crime has also assumed an importance it lacked in earlier years. Much of the interest was fueled by the political scandals of Watergate, but even before those sordid events federal prosecutors had begun to focus on white-collar offenders.[5] Both corporate wrongdoing, in the form of price-fixing and illegal payments abroad, and a variety of individual white-collar crimes, from bribery and embezzlement to securities fraud and tax evasion, received attention from authorities.[6] White-collar crime became a priority for prosecution during the Carter administration and has remained so, at least in Justice Department policy statements, during the regimes of his successor.[7] The best evidence of the growth of this concern is the emergence of a new lawyers' specialty, white-collar crime defense work, a type of practice that a quarter of a century ago employed few people but that has now grown into a substantial form of law practice.[8]

This awakening of interest does not mean that there is a cultural consensus about white-collar crime, or for that matter a consensus with respect to legal and social policy. The fact that such crimes are nonviolent leads some to downplay their significance. In his influential book *Thinking About Crime*, political scientist James Q. Wilson devotes scant attention to white-collar crime, arguing that crimes of violence and invasion of space and property are the true destroyers of community.[9] But white-collar crimes are probably *more* significant than street crimes from a purely economic perspective, and such crimes

3. For an exposition of some of the issues involved, see Andrew von Hirsch, "Prediction of Criminal Conduct and Preventive Confinement of Convicted Persons," 21 *Buffalo Law Review* 717–58 (1972).

4. The Comprehensive Crime Control Act of 1984 was enacted as Title II of House Joint Resolution 648, Public Law 98–473. The sentencing provisions are contained in chapter 2 of the Act, known as the Sentencing Reform Act of 1984.

5. Jack Katz, "The Social Movement against White-Collar Crime," *Criminology Review Yearbook*, ed. Egon Bittner and Sheldon L. Messinger, (Beverly Hills, Cal.: Sage, 1980), 2:161–84.

6. Ibid.

7. See statement of D. Lowell Jensen, deputy attorney general, before the Committee on the Judiciary, United States Senate, February 27, 1986.

8. Kenneth Mann, *Defending White-Collar Crime: A Portrait of Attorneys at Work* (New Haven and London: Yale University Press, 1985).

9. New York: Basic Books, 1975.

often have the capacity to weaken trust and faith in the basic institutions of society.

Our inquiry seeks to understand the sentencing of white-collar offenders from the perspective of those who sit in judgment. In this book we describe the ways in which judges think about the sentencing of white-collar crimes: how they construct or interpret the nature of the offense and the character of the offender, what factors they consider in doing this interpretive work and in fixing particular punishments in particular cases, what problems white-collar cases pose for the sentencing judge and how those problems are dealt with. It is our view that the exploration of sentencing in white-collar cases reveals much about the nature of the sentencing process in general.

Our aim in this volume is to extend current thought about sentencing and its underlying rationale. Our own understanding, and the basis of this book, is derived from a series of in-depth, probing interviews with those who are charged with the task of sentencing in the federal system, where most white-collar offenses are prosecuted, namely, federal district court judges. We conducted lengthy interviews with fifty-one judges in seven federal districts, including those with heavy white-collar crime caseloads.[10]

The research strategy was inductive. We did not begin with well-grounded theoretical assumptions. We did not set out to test hypotheses or to validate propositions. Our beginnings were much more modest. We set out to find out how judges went about the task of sentencing and how they dealt with the sentencing of white-collar offenders. The design of the research was oriented toward the production of a "rich description" of the judicial culture of sentencing as

10. Our interviews were conducted in the judges' chambers. In all but a few instances responses were tape-recorded. The shortest interview was 30 minutes, the longest 3 1/4 hours. Prior to the interview, judges were told that their responses would not be attributed to them by name and that the interview transcript would remain confidential. The interviews came primarily from three districts known to have a high proportion of white-collar crime prosecution: southern New York (Manhattan), northern Illinois (Chicago), and central California (Los Angeles). Some geographic variation was provided through interviews in Arizona (Phoenix), Connecticut, eastern Michigan (Detroit), and Washington, D.C. Because the study focused on white-collar crime, we felt that it was more important to interview judges who handle a large number of such cases than it was to select a representative national sample.

expressed in the language of judges. It was only as we began to interpret and analyze the data we had gathered that we began to see connections to larger themes; to see, if you will, the connection between the native categories that judges deploy in speaking about sentencing in general and the sentencing of white-collar offenders in particular, and fundamental questions in jurisprudence. Thus we began with the case as the unit of analysis. Judges, we believed, organized their thinking about sentencing not in terms of a series of abstractions but as a series of reactions to particular cases. Our interpretation of the data involved a movement from talk about cases to a concern with broad issues concerning the construction of a just and effective sentencing system.[11]

In choosing actual rather than hypothetical cases we had the benefit of discrete factual situations from which to draw answers to general questions. While we were equipped with an open-ended interview schedule and a strong sense of significant areas to explore, the interview had its own dynamic depending on the judges' particular orientation to the case or cases discussed. We did not hesitate either to interrupt the judges where seeming inconsistencies appeared or to adopt an "adversarial" stance when appropriate. Our aim throughout was to understand how judges reason about white-collar offenses. Thus what we offer is a portrait of judicial thought regarding sentencing, a portrait undoubtedly colored by the fact that the judges are explaining

11. The data that we gathered and interpreted is, at the lowest level, just talk. What we present in subsequent chapters is the way in which judges talk to outsiders about sentencing and about the sanctioning of white-collar offenders. We do not pretend that our data map the full intricacies of the ways in which judges think. What we present is a picture of a picture; an interpretation of the ways judges interpret and speak about one part of their job. After extensive analysis of our conversations with judges and a careful review of other studies of sentencing, we are convinced that the accounts provided by the judges are plausible accounts of the major factors that judges are aware of as they sentence offenders. We cannot, of course, be sure that we were not taken in, that we were not presented the official view. Perhaps what we document is not a widespread consensus on the factors that guide sentencing decisions but instead a widespread consensus among judges about the proper way to speak to outsiders. Moreover, we are aware of a kind of parallel process between the social activity of sentencing and the construction of the accounts in this book. In chapter 2 we describe sentencing in terms of an active process of information acquisition and interpretation in which judges put together a portrait of offense and offender. Our task has, of course, run a similar course involving an active gathering of information and interpretation in which we put together a portrait of ways judges talk about sentencing and the connection between that talk and issues in the jurisprudence and practice of sentencing.

their actions after the fact. But whatever its weaknesses, our interview data provide us with the fullest account to date of how judges talk about what they do when they sentence people. We are concerned in this study with judicial thought rather than action. Although we believe our study would be of value in documenting the ways judges verbally legitimize their decisions even if their words were unrelated to their deeds, a companion study shows convincingly that many of the variables described as important by the judges actually do explain variations in sentences meted out in federal courts. Thus we have reason to believe that to an important degree, what judges say is also what they do.[12]

White-Collar Crime vs Common Crime

Since we often refer to white-collar crime and contrast it to common crime, a word about our choice of words is called for. The concept of white-collar crime has carried many meanings.[13] For our purposes the central ingredients are that they are nonviolent, economic crimes that involve some level of fraud, collusion, or deception and that are committed by persons in traditionally "white-collar" jobs. We distinguish them from organized crime on grounds that the latter typically involves force or the threat of force. Concretely, the crimes we have in mind include bribery, income tax fraud, postal and wire fraud, price-fixing, false claims and statements, and bank embezzlement. Because our focus is on understanding the sentencing of individuals and particularly the choice between incarceration and probation, crimes and associated sanctions against corporations and other organizations are not included.[14]

We often contrast judicial views of white-collar crime sentencing with that of "common crime" defendants. We intentionally choose the concept of common crime and the connotation of "common crim-

12. See Stanton Wheeler, David Weisburd, and Nancy Bode, "Sentencing the White Collar Offender: Rhetoric and Reality," *American Sociological Review* 47, no. 4 (Oct. 1982):641–59.

13. Stanton Wheeler, "White Collar Crime: History of An Idea," in *Encyclopedia of Crime and Justice* (New York: Free Press, 1983), 4:1652–56.

14. See John Coffee, " 'No Soul to Damn; No Body to Kick': An Unscandalized Inquiry into the Problem of Corporate Punishment," 70 *Michigan Law Review* 386–459 (1981). See also Kip Schlegel, "Desert and the Allocation of Punishments for Corporations and Their Agents" (Ph.D. diss., Rutgers University, 1987).

inal" rather than the category of "street crime" because the latter more often invokes the notion of fear of possible physical attacks. Judges of course do distinguish between violent crimes and others, but they also distinguish white-collar offenders from non-white-collar offenders who commit such economic crimes as mail theft, forgery of stolen government welfare checks, and the like. The common crime label is applicable to the whole range of offenses typically committed by those who lack the status or position of the white-collar offender.

The Role of the Judge in
White-Collar Sentencing

Why, one might ask, should we be interested in the roles and attitudes of judges in sentencing white-collar offenders? The judge is, after all, but one part of the system for sanctioning convicted criminals, a system in which prosecutors, probation departments, and parole boards (at least until recently) play an important part. While judges have the formal, legal power to impose sentence, their decisions are heavily influenced by the need to accommodate the desires and interests of other participants in the criminal justice system.

Sentencing in State Courts

Skepticism about the significance of the judge as a focus for an inquiry about sentencing is, to some extent, the product of a portrait of the sentencing process derived from studies of common crime in state courts with heavy caseloads in which routinized, mass processing of cases is the norm.[15] Those studies emphasize the highly bureaucratized quality of urban criminal courts and the importance placed on moving the business by doing justice quickly in a system dominated by shared understanding among major participants. The central device for moving the business is the negotiated plea of guilty.[16]

15. James Eisenstein and Herbert Jacob, *Felony Justice* (Boston: Little, Brown, 1977); Robert Dawson, *Sentencing* (Boston: Little, Brown, 1969); Abraham Blumberg, *Criminal Justice* (Chicago: Quadrangle Books, 1967).
16. Suzann R. Thomas-Buckle and Leonard Buckle, *Bargaining for Justice* (New York: Praeger, 1977), and Arthur Rosett and Donald Cressey, *Justice by Consent* (Philadelphia: Lippincott, 1976).

In the typical mass justice state court the central actor is the prosecutor, not the judge, and the line between the guilt determination phase and the sentencing phase is far from clear. In most ordinary cases the issue of guilt or innocence is hardly an issue at all.[17] Once arrested and charged, the defendant typically is interested not so much in trying to get off as in trying to get off as lightly as possible.[18] Thus, almost from the start the focus of the criminal process is on the nature of the punishment to be meted out. This concern sets the agenda of the negotiation, the major subject of which is the effort to determine what the case "is worth" through an agreed upon construction of the events surrounding the crime and the circumstances of the defendant's involvement.[19] This construction of the case proceeds, in most common crimes, rather rapidly as neither the crime nor the defendant's involvement are typically very complicated.[20] Prosecution and defense work jointly, if not with entire cooperation, to come to a shared understanding of crime and criminal.[21] Adversariness lurks in the background but is not, in most cases, part of the day-to-day work of lower criminal courts.

In routine common crimes, the major participants have a clear understanding of the "going rates" for different offenses such that there may be little explicit bargaining over sentencing.[22] Once the case is understood to be of a particular type the translation to an amount of punishment may be virtually automatic. In most state courts, the penalty schedule tends to be relatively fixed and stable with the effort directed toward a rapid categorization of the case, a categorization designed to determine where in the schedule of penalties any particular case actually falls.[23]

Where in all of this is the judge? The judge in state courts is a far less active and dominant figure in the sentencing process than one

17. Lynn Mather, *Plea Bargaining or Trial?* (Lexington, Mass.: Lexington Books, 1979).
18. Jonathan Casper, *American Criminal Justice: The Defendant's Perspective* (Englewood Cliffs, N.J.: Prentice-Hall, 1972).
19. Malcolm Feeley, *The Process Is the Punishment* (New York: Russell Sage, 1979).
20. David Sudnow, "Normal Crimes," *Social Problems* 12 (1965): 255.
21. Blumberg, *Criminal Justice*, and Jackson Battle, "In Search of the Adversary System," 50 *Texas Law Review* 60 (1971).
22. Feeley, *The Process Is the Punishment.*
23. Maureen Mileski, "Courtroom Encounters," 5 *Law and Society Review* 473 (1971).

might suspect given his formal legal powers. While the judge retains the exclusive legal authority to impose sentences, he is generally neither directly involved in the construction and interpretation of the facts of the case nor does he give individualized attention to the cases brought forward for sentencing.[24] Indeed, it is sometimes argued that in systems of bargained justice the sentencing function is effectively and completely transferred from judge to prosecutor.[25]

Sentencing in Federal Courts

A very different and equally salient image of sentencing and of the judge's role in sentencing is drawn from analysis of the federal system, which has nothing like the docket and caseload pressures of state criminal courts.[26] By comparison federal courts are both rich in resources and professionalized. Much of the informal courtroom culture and common ethos, norms, and expectations found in state criminal courts is therefore diluted. In this environment the judge appears to be a more central actor in the sentencing process.

What is generally true for the role of federal court judges is especially true for white-collar crime cases. Even with their greater resources and professionalism, federal judges deal in quantity with common crime defendants in drug cases, robbery cases, interstate movement of stolen vehicles, and the theft or forgery of government checks. In these areas, something akin to going rates found in state courts may operate. But the white-collar cases that occur with some frequency in federal courts are a heterogeneous lot that make simple construction of the central features of a case difficult. Rather than categorizing the case as an instance of a general type routinely handled by the court, judges often feel they must examine closely the characteristics of offense and offender in order to understand the nature of the case before them. Judges learn, to be sure, from how the case

24. Feeley, *The Process Is the Punishment*; Milton Heumann, *Plea Bargaining* (Chicago: University of Chicago Press, 1977); John Paul Ryan and James Alfini, "The Judge's Participation in Plea Bargaining," 13 *Law and Society Review* 479 (Winter 1979).

25. James Cramer et al., "The Judicial Role in Plea Bargaining," in *Plea Bargaining*, ed. James Cramer and William McDonald (Lexington, Mass.: Lexington Books, 1980).

26. Given state systems as varied as those in the U.S., any blanket comparison is dangerous. Some state courts, such as those in New York, New Jersey, and California, may be as well equipped in personnel and resources as the federal system, but most are not.

is treated by prosecution and defense, but they more often retain their own authority to decide on the sentence, rarely letting it fall into a simple going rate category, and less often acquiescing in judgment agreed to by prosecution and defense attorney.

In this kind of a system, there is every reason to treat the judge as a central actor—indeed *the* most central actor—in the sentencing process. It is the judge, ultimately, who will make the fateful decision among probation, fine, imprisonment, or some combination and whose sentence in the case of imprisonment will influence the length of time served, even where a paroling authority has the last word. Thus it is not surprising that in the federal system reports on sentencing have been closely tied to judges and their views. Indeed, the most influential report on federal sentencing in the past two decades was the work of a judge, Marvin Frankel.[27]

The Common Understanding
about Federal Sentencing

Frankel's account of federal sentencing was important in part because it expressed the views of a sitting judge, but it was not the only expression of such views. Indeed, most studies of the period came to conclusions similar to those reported in Frankel's book.[28] The Frankel account gives voice to four central points that might be called the common understanding about federal sentencing that was shared by most commentators as the decade of the 1980s began.

First, *sentencing systems allow a vast amount of discretion.* Judge Frankel speaks of the "almost wholly unchecked and sweeping powers we give to judges in the fashioning of sentences."[29] His examples, drawn from the federal system, are even less extreme than might have been found in some of our states, but the federal reality seems bad enough. Referring to the maximum penalty of not more than five years for postal theft, the judge notes that federal trial judges, "an-

27. *Criminal Sentences: Law without Order* (New York: Hill and Wang. 1973).
28. Anthony Partridge and William B. Eldridge, *A Report to the Judges of the Second Circuit* (Washington, D.C.: Federal Judicial Center, 1974). See also Pierce O'Donnell, Michael J. Churgin, and Dennis E. Curtis, *Toward a Just and Effective Sentencing System* (New York: Praeger, 1977).
29. Frankel, *Criminal Sentences*, 5.

swerable only to their varieties of conscience," may send people to prison for terms "that may vary in any given case from none at all up to five, ten, thirty or more years."[30] The range in the allowable sanction for any given statutory offense becomes, then, one of the principal critiques in the common understanding.

In noting that the judges are answerable "only to their varieties of conscience," Judge Frankel prepares us for a second basic proposition: *There are no agreed upon principles underlying the structure of sentencing.* Even though some minimal consensus on the legitimate purposes of sentencing has been reached—the usual litany includes deterrence, incapacitation, rehabilitation, and some form of either "desert" or "retribution"—there are no standards by which these purposes can be graded and combined in individual cases.

This absence of clearly specified criteria might not pose such a problem if judges approached the task of sentencing with like minds, tastes, and aptitudes, but they do not, and this produces a third basic proposition: *In the absence of agreed upon standards, judges will give vent to their own ideologies, their own sentiments and values.* Judge Frankel devotes chapter 2 of his book on sentencing to "individualized judges" and documents how disparate they are, how little training or preparation they have for the task of sentencing, what varied backgrounds they bring to their role as sentencing judge. Sometimes the emphasis may be placed upon the potential for class or racial bias, and other times on the essentially random process that may place one convicted defendant before a lenient judge and another before a "hanging" judge. The idea that the enormous discretion may be expressed in so many different forms and degrees is intolerable to a system that proclaims governance under the rule of law.

These three propositions lead to a fourth and final one: *There is massive disparity in sentences.* The consequence is injustice to those sentenced and to our conception of legitimate order and authority. Those who have examined the evidence, though they may agree that it is often anecdotal, are convinced that disparity is one of the most well-established features of our sentencing systems. It is precisely a review of that evidence that led O'Donnell et al. to the conclusion that sentencing is a "national scandal."[31]

---

30. Ibid., 6.
31. O'Donnell, Churgin, and Curtis, *Toward a Just Sentencing System.*

Disparity and Principles in Sentencing

This consensus on the existence and the evils of disparity is striking. Rarely, in sentencing, as in criminal justice generally, is there consensus among authorities on much of anything. Indeed, one would probably have to go back to the turn of the century to find a similar unanimity of view among those who count. Eugene Smith, the president of the Prison Association of New York, wrote in 1907,

> The Indeterminate sentence is so logically reasonable, so easy of comprehension and so commends itself to common intelligence, that it has, within a few years, secured wide adoption. It is now firmly incorporated in the penal systems of about one-third of the states of the union, comprising those of the greatest power and influence. There is no longer need of argument in support of the indeterminate sentence....[32]

> The old theory of retributive punishment, [wrote Mr. Smith,] has been thoroughly discredited and is now repudiated by all competent authorities.... The main function of government is the protection of the people from injustice, damage, and wrong. The state imprisons a convict because it is not safe for the same reasons that detain in quarantine a ship bearing contagion; it is a protective measure holding at bay what is a menace and a danger to the community. If this theory is correct, it follows that the imprisonment should continue as long as the danger lasts.[33]

It is ironic that the view "so logically reasonable" at the turn of the century should have become the basis for "a national scandal" three-quarters of a century later.[34] This stark fact should make us at least

32. "The Indeterminate Sentence for Crime—Its Use and Abuse," in *Sixty-Second Annual Report of the Prison Association of New York* (Albany: J. B. Lyon 1907), 65.

33. Ibid., 64.

34. The introduction of the indeterminate sentence was not always an effort to express a rehabilitative philosophy. Sheldon Messinger and his colleagues have examined the origins of indeterminacy through parole in California and found that judges there had considerable discretion under the earlier determinate sentencing systems and that disparity was a problem for them. "The true irony," he writes in a personal communication, "is that indeterminacy, in the form of parole, was initially adopted in part to *reduce* disparity by centralizing the decision about length of term." See Sheldon L. Messinger, John E. Berecochea, David Rauma, and Richard A. Berk, "The Foundations of Parole in California," 19 *Law and Society Review* 69–106 (1985).

mildly skeptical of any consensus of views reported today, including consensus on the problem of disparity. Yet it is precisely such a consensus that produced the support for a new Sentencing Commission that would reduce disparity through a system of guidelines. How accurate is the consensus? It is hard to tell. Most students of the subject are convinced that the disparity is real, but they are less certain about what produces it.[35] The most thorough review of the vast literature on sentencing, one conducted by a panel appointed by the National Academy of Sciences, concludes that "the evidence for sentence disparity is extensive, but data on the sources of that disparity are scarce."[36] The same study notes, however, that variables like seriousness of offense and prior record show up consistently as predictors of severity of sanctions.[37] Certainly many of the correlates of sentence severity, in recent studies based on federal data, suggest some rationality to the system.[38] But whatever the level of disparity, it is important to understand how judges think and reason as they employ their discretion in the setting of sentences. With occasional exceptions, the studies of sentencing tell us more about outcomes than about process, and

35. Unfortunately, one study that was widely circulated and helped give credence to the notion of rampant disparity did so in part through a misleading presentation of evidence. The aforementioned report of the Second District Sentencing Study shows how judges, in case after hypothetical case, differ in the sentences they would give. What the researchers do not show, but what is apparent in a reanalysis of their data, is that the judges are in rather remarkable agreement on the *rank ordering* of the cases in terms of severity. The coefficient of concordance among the rankings of judges was + .81, suggesting that they are in heated agreement about which cases generally deserve the more severe sentence. The disparity is not on which case is more serious, but on what sanction should be attached to a less serious and a more serious case.

36. Alfred Blumstein, Jacqueline Cohen, Susan E. Martin, and Michael Tonry, eds., *Research on Sentencing: The Search for Reform* (Washington, D.C.: National Academy Press, 1983), 123. See also John Hagen, Ilene H. Nagel, and Celesta Albonetti, "The Differential Sentencing of White Collar Offenders in the Federal Courts," *American Sociological Review* 45 (1980):802–20. Shari Seidman Diamond has explored the sources of disparity; we discuss her work in chapter 6.

37. Blumstein et al., *Research on Sentencing*, 83–85.

38. Wheeler, Weisburd, and Bode, "Sentencing the White-Collar Offender," 641–59. For a different but not conflicting view, see Ilene H. Nagel and John L. Hagen, "The Sentencing of White Collar Criminals in Federal Courts: A Socio-Legal Explanation of Disparity," 80 *Michigan Law Review* 1427–65 (June 1982).

since much of that process goes on in the head of the judge, it is essential to explore judges' thinking in depth and detail if we are to understand the basis for their actions.[39]

We have made that exploration. What we have found partially corroborates the common understanding discussed earlier, but it also suggests a significant departure. In the chapters that follow, we describe what we learned from our interviews with the judges, letting them speak in their own voices as much as possible. The judges, as they and any who work with them will say, are individuals, and each expresses her or his views in their own language, their own tongue, derived from years of experience—in life if not always on the bench. But the striking thing to us is that those individual voices yield a portrait of judging and of the elements that go into sentencing that suggest a rather more substantial sharing of views than is suggested by the "common understanding." Further, this sharing can be seen to reflect a pattern of thought about sentencing that has deep roots in the Anglo-American legal system. It suggests an agreement on principles that is greater than that proposed in current accounts. But that agreement does not produce uniformity in actual sentences. The reasons it does not are in some cases well known, in others not. Taken together, these findings suggest that we should make some alterations in our thinking about sentencing, alterations that have practical consequences for sentencing systems.

It is the burden of the remaining chapters to provide the detailed evidence, but in the remainder of this chapter we present a distilled version of the argument. One of our aims is to shed new light upon both white-collar crime and sentencing. We think we can do that best by distilling from the interviews the central themes that find broad endorsement and by organizing them into an orderly series of points about sentencing that give expression to what we would call an incipient common law of sentencing. No single judge, of course, spoke of sentencing in just these terms, but if one takes the words of the various judges and distills the common themes, the theory reported in the next few pages (absent the detail provided in later chapters) is the result.

39. For two different exceptions, see John Hogarth, *Sentencing as a Human Process* (Toronto: University of Toronto Press, 1971), and Willard Gaylin, *Partial Justice: A Study of Bias in Sentencing* (New York: Knopf, 1974).

A Theory of Sentencing, with Special
Reference to White-Collar Offenders

The Judge's Task

The task facing the judge at sentencing is to decide what particular sanction among the range of alternatives is to be assigned to the defendant in question. The system invites the judge to differentiate between offenses and offenders, providing more severe sanctions for some and less severe sanctions for others. The judge is implicitly asking the question, Is this the kind of offender and the kind of offense that calls for a sanction near the maximum, near the minimum, or somewhere in between?

The materials that may serve as a basis for the judge's decision vary from case to case and to some extent from court to court. Where the case has gone to trial, the judge may have a vivid sense of the defendant. Where, as in the majority of cases, the defendant has offered a plea of guilty or nolo contendere the judge may have less direct experience. In either case, a very important part of the information that comes to a judge is contained in the pre-sentence investigation conducted for the court by the probation office.

Whatever the total set of materials available to judges, they are not passive recipients of information. They are actively engaged in interpreting the material—in trying to make out what sort of persons are before them. They must decide what aspects of the person and his conduct are to receive greatest consideration in arriving at a sentence. Drawing on their past experience with other cases, on the facts of this particular case, and on the normative lens through which they judge offenders, they actively construct a particular defendant to be the kind of person for whom a particular sanction is justified.

Legal Constraints

Although a wide variety of legal doctrines and opinions and legislative rulings controls the conduct of criminal trials, the sentencing process is remarkably free of such constraints. Federal judges were, at the time of this study, mandated to set sentences within legislatively graded ranges of prison terms and fines (Table 1).

Each of the prison terms shown in the accompanying schedule is a

Table 1. Schedule of Penalties for Selected Federal Crimes

	Maximum Prison Term	Fine
Bankruptcy fraud (18 USC 152)	5 years	$ 5,000
Bribery (18 USC 201)	15 yrs	20,000
Gratuities (18 USC 201)	2 yrs	10,000
Fraudulent Claims (18 USC 287)	5 yrs	10,000
Conspiracy to Defraud U.S. (18 USC 371)	5 yrs	10,000
Embezzlement of Public Funds (18 USC 641) Over $100	10 yrs	10,000
Embezzlement of Public Funds (18 USC 641) Up to $100	1 yr	1,000
Embezzlement of Bank Funds (18 USC 656) Over $100	5 yrs	5,000
Embezzlement of Bank Funds (18 USC 656) Up to $100	1 yr	1,000
False Statement to Government (18 USC 1001)	5 yrs	10,000
Mail Fraud (18 USC 1341)	5 yrs	1,000
Tax Evasion (26 USC 7201)	5 yrs	10,000

maximum term, meaning that the judge (with rare exception) can set any sentence from no term in prison to the maximum. The same principle applies for fines. Within these legislatively defined ranges, there is no other statutory restriction. And offenders may be sentenced on several counts, or, indeed, on several different offenses, on which the court may sentence either concurrently or consecutively.

On its face alone, the exemplary penalty schedule shows that there is a broad range of prison terms, in addition to the no prison option.

Table 1. (cont.)

	Maximum Prison Term	Fine
Failure to File Tax Return (26 USC 7203)	1 yr	10,000
Restraint of Trade (15 USC 1)	3 yrs	$1 million—corporation $100,000–individual
Racketeering: participation in racketeering influenced organization	20 yrs	25,000
Manufacture or distribution of heroin or other specified drugs (21 USC 841)	15 yrs	15,000
Bank robbery by force or violence (18 USC 2113(a))	20 yrs	5,000
Bank theft over $100 (18 USC 2113 (a))	10 yrs	5,000
Bank theft up to $100 (18 USC 2113 (a))	1 yr	1,000
Assault with deadly weapon (18 USC 111)	10 yrs	10,000
Assault (18 USC 111)	3 yrs	5,000
Espionage (18 USC 794)	death or any term of years	

In a system that has no statutory sentencing mandates other than the requirement of setting a term or fine within the ranges defined, and the judge is free not to mete out a prison term or not to set a fine if he or she so chooses, the legislative framework establishes only weakly felt constraints and gives little direction in determining how to set sentences in specific cases.

This interpretation of the penalty schedule depends, of course, on the general normative sense about appropriate sentences held by judges. If the maximum sentences were perceived as too low, the legislative standard would constitute a real constraint on judges. There would be little room for taking account of individual differences in cases and little variation in the actual sentences meted out. Apparent discretion would not be real discretion. Judges do feel such a constraint with fines, where the maximum is often felt to be grossly insufficient. But in regard to prison terms, judges experience almost no constraint from the available maximums.

The Centrality of Actual Conduct

Elements of the charging instrument—an indictment or an information—might seem to serve as a constraint, but for most judges they do not. Most judges believe in taking account of the offenders' total conduct when they pass sentence—what is known as real-offense sentencing.[40] What is alleged in the indictment becomes only the starting point. The typical federal judge is interested (in the words of one of our judges) "in the total picture of what was going on, not in the slice selected by the prosecution for inclusion in the indictment." If the pre-sentence report indicates greater wrongdoing than the indictment, the judge will reflect it in his sentence.

Nor does the number of counts charged in the indictment carry heavy weight at sentencing. Some prosecutors may charge each of a series of false representations as a separate count, while others may lump them together. One must "look behind the charging instrument" to avoid the uneven impact of prosecutorial discretion. Of course, there are exceptions to this general rule—an occasional judge who feels entirely constrained by the indictment, or a judge who would sentence a defendant to two different sentences if he had two counts to work with. But we found that the judges we interviewed were, most of the time, anxious to base their sentence on the real behavior of the defendant in question and not on the vicissitudes of prosecutorial charging decisions. And for this reason, evidence of underlying conduct appearing in the pre-sentence investigation report (or coming to

40. John C. Coffee, Jr., and Michael Tonry, "Hard Choices: Critical Trade-offs in the Implementation of Sentencing Reforms through Guidelines," in *Reform and Punishment: Essays on Criminal Sentencing*, ed. Michael Tonry and Franklin E. Zimring (Chicago: University of Chicago Press, 1983). See also Michael H. Tonry, "Real Offense Sentencing: The Model Sentencing and Corrections Act," 72 *Journal of Criminal Law and Criminology*, 1550 (1981).

light through other means) plays a critical role in determining the actual sentence.

The Distinguishing Feature of White-Collar Cases

When judges confront white-collar cases, their sentencing world is particularly complicated. First, the cases are enormously heterogeneous. It is harder to speak of a typical bribery or securities fraud than of a typical drug deal or mail theft. The documents available to aid judges in sentencing, like the indictment and the pre-sentence investigation report, are more detailed and more complicated. And in white-collar cases, far more often than in common crimes, the very existence of a crime may be in dispute, and matters of intent and motivation are often ambiguous.[41]

Moreover, white-collar cases more often are subject to the adversarial efforts of defense attorneys, a fact that tends to complicate rather than simplify the classification of a case.[42] Defense attorneys regularly seek to relitigate issues of responsibility and intent and to raise questions about the nature of the real offense even after legal responsibility has been admitted or adjudicated. The superior resources of defendants in these cases as well as the nature of their offenses allow defense attorneys to continue arguing, or to reargue, cases on their merits during the sentencing hearing. This may be done through extensive and well-documented sentencing memoranda. The result is to demand the active participation of the judge in making the kind of decisions about offense and offender that in common crimes and particularly at the state level are more often left to negotiations between prosecution and defense. Furthermore, the resources of the federal probation department and the comparatively high quality of the pre-sentence investigation reports they produce give the judge an independent source of information against which to test versions of events presented to him.

Finally, in white-collar cases judges are usually deprived of two of the primary qualities that help the judge decide on a sentence: a violent act and a prior record. White-collar offenses are nonviolent economic

41. Jack Katz, "Legality and Equality: Plea Bargaining in the Prosecution of White-Collar and Common Crimes," 13 *Law and Society Review* 431 (Winter, 1979) 435–39.
42. Mann, *Defending White-Collar Crime.*

crimes, and they are usually committed by persons with little or no prior record of arrests, let alone convictions. In the absence of these two aggravating criteria that customarily identify defendants suited for prison sentences, the central questions arise: How to decide who goes to prison, and for how long? Here sentences will have to be based on qualities of the offense and offender other than violence and prior record. This gives a distinctive quality to the interpretive work the judge must do in arriving at an appropriate sentence.

This was the real-world context of white-collar crime sentencing in the U.S. federal system in the mid-eighties: a judge with broad discretion, focused on the actual conduct of the offender, presented with detailed background material from the pre-sentence report as well as competing versions of the offense and offender shaped adversarily by prosecutor and defense counsel, working to make distinctions among a heterogeneous group of cases without the presence of either violence or prior convictions as relevant criteria for translating a case to a sentence. The question is, How do they do it? Upon what do they base their decisions? How do they think about and justify giving a shorter sentence here, a longer one there, or none at all?

The Normative Lens

Our basic thesis is that judges apply a common normative lens to the task of sentencing, a normative lens that has a rich tradition in Anglo-American law and cultural experience. The normative lens through which judges view the cases is neither so varied nor idiosyncratic as is commonly believed. There is a broad consensus, across a wide range of judges of otherwise different temperaments and styles, on the core principles that ought to be applied in the sentencing of offenders. It is not a mechanical agreement. Particular judges in particular types of cases may be at a far remove from the general consensus. But this should not blind us to an agreement on the most general and basic principles.

At the heart of this common moral lens lie three core legal norms that are deeply rooted in the history of Anglo-American jurisprudence. The first is the norm that offenses should be treated differently according to the *harm* they produce. Again and again, judges struggle with the notion of harm, or damage, or loss, or injury, usually to

particular victims, sometimes to the system itself. The consequence
of the offense is central to judges' thinking about sentence. *How*
harmful, *how* damaging, *how* destructive was the act? The norm of
harm finds its primary legal expression in the legislative grading of
crimes. It is one of the oldest and most deeply rooted values in our
legal system—that people should be judged by the amount of harm
or damage they do.

In assessing harm, judges are not limited to harm as it is defined in
one or another section of the criminal code, for instance, "deprivation
of revenue to the treasury." They work with an *expanded conception*
of harm that may include matters (like amount of loss) that are also
reflected in legislative grading, but they may also include matters (like
duration of offense or whether the victim was an individual or an
organization) that are often only implicit, if that, in legislation.

The second principle is the norm of *blameworthiness*: Offenders
should be treated differently according to the blameworthiness of their
actions. As with harm, judges found it virtually impossible to discuss
a case without some assessment of the moral culpability of the offender. Some spoke bluntly ("You have to realize this was really a
bad guy— thoroughly corrupt and dishonest") while others were less
direct. The consistency with which their concern returned to assessment of the elements of the moral character of offenders convinces
us that it lies at the heart of judicial thought.

The legal base of blameworthiness is typically found in the common-
law cases that establish the conditions for the assignment of criminal
responsibility. Judges do not work with a narrow, technical sense of
blameworthiness. Rather, they work with an expanded conception of
this crucial legal norm that enables them to bring into play considerations that typically escape attention in case law. But this expanded
conception still has at its core a set of ideas that have been the foundation of our legal order for centuries.

The conventional elements of criminal intent that are essential to
establishing grounds for conviction in a criminal case are often the
starting point for a judge's consideration of blameworthiness. But this
consideration usually reaches beyond the starting point to include a
broader moral sphere. That sphere may reach into the earlier history
of the defendant, into the details of the defendant's role in the crime,
into a character assessment based on how the defendant reacted to
the fact of arrest and conviction, or into whether the defendant was

moved by need or by greed, matters rarely relevant for purposes of guilt determination. The broad general principle of blameworthiness encompasses all of them.

The two norms of harm and blameworthiness are often joined to provide a kind of foundation for sentencing: together they allow a judge to assess the *seriousness of a case*. Judges speak of cases, by which they typically mean a combination of a particular offense (and its associated social harm) and a particular offender (and associated blameworthiness). The seriousness of a case provides the central normative bedrock or resting point for sentencing.

Although the moral forces of judgments of harm and blameworthiness sometimes pull in opposite directions—a petty offense by a habitual criminal, a major economic crime by a first offender— some qualities seem to adhere both to the offense and the offender. One of these qualities is especially significant in white-collar cases: the violation of trust. When persons in positions of significant financial or public trust violate that trust in the commission of crimes, they add both to the harm done—by threatening the fabric of trust on which transactions in the society are often based— and to the blameworthiness of the defendant—by adding to his criminal responsibility the added moral opprobrium that attaches to one who lets others down by violating the trust placed in him. Thus, the most serious of white-collar crimes are often judged to be those in which huge economic gains are made at the expense of trusting victims.

One reason for judges' close attention to norms of harm and blameworthiness appears to be their concern for justice, fairness, and equity in sentencing. Just as it is unjust to sanction persons at all unless they meet minimal standards of the criminal law founded on harm and blameworthiness, they feel it is unjust to sanction persons differently unless they differ in the harm or the blameworthiness of their conduct. But judges are also concerned with harm and blameworthiness because they are indicators of the degree of injury to the society and therefore communicate to the judge the level of deterrent force that should be used in preventing others from committing similar crimes. For our judges, if there is primarily a "just deserts" concern behind their examination of harm and blameworthiness, there is also a utilitarian concern. In cases of white-collar crime, as in other crimes, greater harm brings greater punishment in order to provide greater protection to society. But greater blameworthiness, or a more vicious will, as some would say, is also a measure of the degree of injury caused to society. A carefully planned fraud committed with stealth and cover-up must warrant more punishment because it causes greater injury to the citizens' sense of security.

As important as the twin norms of harm and blameworthiness are, they do not exhaust judges' views about sentences. A third principle is that of *consequence*. This principle—that judges should consider the consequences of their sanction in choosing one—also has a long history, though perhaps one less deeply rooted in traditional legal thought. The primary social consequence in the judge's view is deterrence or general prevention. Judges worry much about the message they are implicitly sending to the community by virtue of the sanction they give. They often find it difficult to elevate the concern for deterrence to the level granted judgments about the harm caused by the offense and the blameworthiness of the offender, and they find it difficult to sanction for general deterrence purposes alone, if they cannot also justify that sanction on grounds of moral culpability or gravity of offense. Nevertheless, especially in white-collar cases, general deterrence is a most relevant consequence.

Concern for deterrence is a generalized element of consequence affecting the whole society. A second element of consequence is more personal. It asks, What will be the effect of the sanction on the person sanctioned, or on his or her immediate family or work associates? Because white-collar offenders are often new to the criminal justice system, because their families often have status in the community, because these offenders are often employers whose own workers will suffer if they are imprisoned, the personal as well as the societal effects of the sanction loom large in white-collar cases.

Consequence is no more easily reduced to a measurable phenomenon than harm or blameworthiness, containing as it does both broad societal aspects like deterrence and the potentially enormous variety of individual consequences for defendant and those with significant relationships to the defendant. Indeed, its diverse elements more often pull in opposite directions than the indicators of harm and blameworthiness. But it is a norm (or series of norms) that appears in almost every judge's account of why they sentence as they do, and along with harm and blameworthiness completes the foundation of judicial reflection and judgment about the sentencing of offenders.

Institutionalization of Common Cultural Norms

The foregoing description of judicial practice draws on the self-accounted experience of the judges rather than on jurisprudential arguments set out independent of actual cases. The normative lens we have been able to describe grows out of the accumulated but undocumented case-by-case experience of judges. In a sense, judges have told us what they might have written had there been a requirement of giving written reasons in the sentencing process. What we learn is that judges appear to have created, on their own, a kind of common law of sentencing—without real legislative guidance and without a system of judicial precedent on which to rely.

One way of capturing what these judges are doing is by borrowing and altering a concept from legal anthropology known as the institutionalization of legal norms. The anthropologist Paul James Bohanon, in an important article some years ago, argued that the legal system takes norms already institutionalized in the general culture—social norms for which there is a relatively broad consensus—and by converting them into formal laws gives those norms a *double institutionalization*.[43] Our argument is that judges in white-collar cases, rather than bringing in novel considerations and new theories, are engaging in yet a further level of institutionalization of the basic normative order.

It is a further institutionalization of the norm demanding that harms be punished, and a specification of it in a particular case, that the judges are engaged in when they assess the social harm of the offender's conduct. Similarly, it is a reinstitutionalization of the basic norm of criminal responsibility, though in expanded form, that the judges are engaged in when they consider the blameworthiness of the offender. Though they may use different terminology and may differ in degrees of subtlety of expression and of interpretation there is a common core of thought that characterizes a wide array of judges. That common core is drawn from central legal norms that themselves are reflections of historically rooted cultural values. Application of those norms to particular offenders gives the norms an additional level of institutionalization in the sense that Bohanon spoke of it.

43. "The Differing Realms of Law," in *Law and Warfare: Studies in the Anthropology of Conflict*, ed. Paul Bohanon (New York: Natural History Press, 1967), 43–56.

In a fully developed legal system, the combination of legislation and common-law decisions would provide a structure, a set of standards that would guide judicial discretion. As critics point out, at least until recently, this guidance has been largely absent in sentencing.[44] Statutes define crimes and specify a broad range of penalties, but they do not provide specific guidelines for choosing within the range of penalties. Nor is case law well developed. This is why the area has the appearance of being lawless. In their search for principles of sentencing judges reach back, as it were, to the cultural norms from which both legislation and case law are drawn. Underlying their commonsense judgments is a broad normative base formed in part, to be sure, by legal conceptions, but also by more general concepts that are embedded in the culture.

The accompanying diagram suggests the basic relationships.

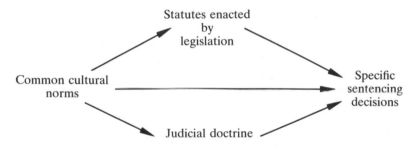

The judges begin with the framework provided by legislation and case law, but that framework lacks, or lacked until the recent period, the kind of detail that would compel and give reasons for specific sentencing decisions. In its absence judges, in effect, reach back through the legislation and case law to the underlying principles, sometimes adding, embellishing, expanding the notions embedded in those principles, but staying close enough to them to provide at least a minimally coherent framework for sentencing. The result is an unwritten, informal common law of sentencing.

Deciding on an Actual Sentence

If this common law of sentencing provided a method for translating principles of sentencing into discrete decisions, we might not have the

---

44. See Gaylin, *Partial Justice*, and Frankel, *Criminal Sentences*.

sense of disarray that is found in the criminal justice system. But generalized agreement on principles does not lead inevitably to a consensus in actual practice. There are critical methodological and conceptual problems in applying the norms. Although judges broadly agree on general principles, they do not have similar agreement either on ways of measuring or assessing the principles or on the relative weighting to be given each or on the translation of a given weighting into an actual sentence. This may be attributed in part to the absence of a jurisprudence that ties the principles systematically to discrete outcomes.

Even if the jurisprudence were complete, other differences might still lead to great disparity in outcome absent some authoritative requirement to move from the principles to a discrete sentence in a defined manner. There are differences in the social contexts of judging as well as in the personal styles of judges that would complicate any translation of principle into practice. There are individual differences in judges' response to publicity, in their degree of empathy with white-collar offenders, in their sensitivity to what is happening in courtrooms other than their own. There are also organizational differences in the facilities available in different districts, in how much judges share in the sentencing decisions of their colleagues, and in how each district relates to its local environment.

What happens, then, is that the general agreement on the basic principles underlying sentencing does not produce consensus on actual sentences. Our assessment of the common understanding discussed earlier is that it is basically correct (though perhaps overdrawn) in pointing to disparity but wrong in attributing that disparity to conflict or chaos in the nature of the underlying principles. We found an analytically sophisticated set of basic principles to be prominent in the commonsense judgments and opinions of federal judges. Disarray could not then be a by-product of the absence of principles. It is more directly connected to the problem of translating the principles into consistent sentences, especially where multiple principles may conflict. We suggest, as we will elaborate on in the concluding chapter, that part of the solution to the disparity problem lies in developing a jurisprudence for translation and a mechanism for making that jurisprudence obligatory for the sentencing judge.

We think the basic principles described here, and most particularly the degree to which they are shared by sentencing judges, have been

LIBRARY OF MOUNT ST. MARY'S COLLEGE EMMITSBURG, MARYLAND

lost sight of in all the concern over judicial bias, unfettered discretion, and the play of individual differences in sentencing. By examining judges' views closely we are in a better position to locate and describe the elements that feed both the consensus and the dissensus. Finally, we are able to spell out at least a few of the consequences that flow from our assessment and to make them part of the discussion of the choices faced by those who are designing and implementing new sentencing systems.

■ 2

The Process of Criminal Sentencing

Sentencing decisions require judges to obtain and assess a great deal of information. The way in which that information is presented as well as its detail and content is critical in the shaping of sentences. For the most part judges receive information prepared and presented by others. While their wishes, needs, or decisional styles may influence that preparation and presentation, the judge is rarely able to obtain all the information he might find desirable in making sentencing decisions. The incompleteness of the information along with its volume and complexity contributes substantially to the difficulty of the decisional task.

Sentencing in federal courts may be understood in part as an informational process, with the judge as the receiver and with others seeking to manage his impressions. As John Hogarth argues, sentencing is "a cognitive process in which information concerning the offender, the offense and the surrounding circumstances is read, organized in relation to other information and integrated into an overall assessment of the case."[1] Sentencing is structured by the distinctive modes in which information is presented as well as by the characteristic ways in which particular judges respond to it. Both the mode of presentation and the style of response tend to be predictable, the former by the routines of court custom and practice, the latter by the patterns of information use that judges bring to their decision-making responsibilities.

In our view the informational activities and processes central to sentencing have three basic traits. First, *the core of the informational*

1. *Sentencing as a Human Process* (Toronto: University of Toronto Press, 1971), 279.

basis of sentencing is highly routinized and regularized. This is not to
say that all courts and judges receive the same information or follow
the same procedures in sentencing. Some employ formal pre-sentence
hearings, others do not; some participate with other judges in sentencing councils, others do not; some invite sentencing memoranda
from prosecutors and defense attorneys, others do not. But routinely,
the judge will be exposed to the indictment or information that serves
as the official version of the offense and to the pre-sentence report,
which provides basic background information on the convicted defendant and sometimes additional detail on the nature of the offense.
While details of the pre-sentence report vary from district to district
and are often tailored by request of the judge, the basic form and
content are stable.

Judges have a regular expectation that they will receive the detailed
information provided in the pre-sentence report, and they adapt their
decisional modes and styles to the timing and substance of that report.
Many assume a passive role and limit their search for information to
that which is routinely provided by the pre-sentence report; indeed,
some are resistant to other informational modes.

Second, *the information process at sentencing is pluralistic.* There
are many channels through which information may be communicated,
some of which are geared especially for the sentencing decision, some
of which are not. Each of the sources of information upon which judges
rely has its own angle of vision, none of which is necessarily that of
the judge. What this means is that the judge must see through the
lenses of others. The judges with whom we talked rarely suggested
that any one source of information could be counted on to be totally
impartial. This includes the pre-sentence report provided by the probation department. From the plural and biased sources of information
available to him, the judge must construct a picture or an impression
of the offense and the offender that satisfies his own criteria of completeness. This picture or impression is a social construction of a complex event and a detailed life history.

Third, *the information process is often adversarial.* We have not only
pluralistic voices, but voices representing directly opposing interests—
those of the state and those of the accused. The way the adversarial
nature of the process affects the information flow colors all aspects of
the case. What really happened? Prosecution and defense are likely

to have different versions of the facts.[2] What meaning should we assign to what happened? Again, the adversarial process is likely to lead to opposing interpretations of reality. What is the legal status of the behavior in question? Defense and prosecution may have sharply differing views.

Each of these basic traits is significant in itself, and each is in tension with the others. Routinization allows for and encourages the passive role of judges in information acquisition, yet pluralism encourages an active, interpretive, synthetic approach to the information. Adversariness invites the judge to be more arbiter and less interpreter.

The Sources of Information

The Indictment

Judges often first become aware of what a case is about by reading the indictment. The indictment provides an official statement of the specific violations of law that the government has decided to charge. It not only informs the judge of the offense by citing a statutory section, but also provides a description of the elements of the crime, including particularly the behavior of the defendant that constitutes the subject of the criminal charge. Through the use of separate counts, the indictment may also divide the behavior of the defendant into separate transactions and separate instances of victimization, alleging that more than one offense was committed. This information gives the judge a rudimentary sense of the nature of the case before him. It also provides a basic guide for the judge in his determination of how to sentence the convicted defendant. On the other hand, and equally important, the substance of the indictment may restrict the judge's view of the case: it may not include, for example, facts that constitute a separate crime committed by the defendant or that would aggravate the seriousness of the crime already charged. Moreover, behavior that could have been charged as a felony may be charged under a misdemeanor section, a charging decision that will clearly restrict the judge in his sentencing alternatives.

The indictment is, of course, the government's document. Indict-

2. Malcolm Feeley, *The Process Is the Punishment* (New York: Russell Sage, 1979).

ments vary in their strategy of presentation. It is said that the government sometimes encourages the grand jury to include in the indictment all counts for which there is any shred of reliable evidence even though some counts may be unprovable. This strategy provides something to give away should plea bargaining occur. It also allows the government to shape the initial thinking of the judge as to what the case is about. In complex or difficult cases, however, the government may move to indict on only the strongest evidence and, in so doing, to present the impression of an ironclad case.

The extent to which the indictment constitutes a significant source of information about the case will depend on two important variables in the sentencing process: Does the judge's sense of appropriate legal doctrine require that he exclude from consideration crimes or other wrongful behavior not charged in the indictment? What other sources of information are available that may complete or change the picture of the crime charged in the indictment?

In the introductory chapter, we stated that the judges we interviewed overwhelmingly favored real-offense sentencing.[3] This means, as we have explained already, that the judge is interested in assessing the true nature of the defendant and his illegal behavior and is not particularly concerned about limiting himself or herself to the "four corners" of the charge. Where this view prevails, the indictment is likely to have only a minor role as a source of information. This is a result of the fact that judges will want to go behind the indictment to discover the real characteristics of the case.

The importance of the judge's view on real-offense sentencing is made more vivid by an examination of an exception to this general rule. One of the judges interviewed took the view that real-offense sentencing improperly compromises due process values, in particular the principle that the state must prove, beyond a reasonable doubt, all facts detrimental to a defendant. This judge had been subject to sharp criticism when he decided to restrict himself to sentencing solely on the indictment in a serious fraud case that had received substantial pre-sentence publicity. The defendant had pleaded guilty to one count

---

3. See John C. Coffee, Jr., and Michael Tonry, "Hard Choices: Critical Trade-offs in the Implementation of Sentencing Reforms through Guidelines," in *Reform and Punishment: Essays on Criminal Sentencing*, ed. Michael Tonry and Franklin E. Zimring (Chicago: University of Chicago Press, 1983).

of a multicount indictment pursuant to a plea agreement. Commenting on the case, the judge said,

It was agreed that each of the attorneys would give me whatever materials in connection with the sentence they thought was pertinent. Well, the government came in with a long memorandum, discussing the other nine-tenths of the indictment [not pled to as a result of the plea bargain], and the defendant's lawyer came in with a massive amount of material trying to rebut that so they were trying to have a trial on memos of nine-tenths of the indictment. It was utterly unsatisfactory, and I worked very hard on that. It was a very difficult sentence. There were lots of other things about his personal circumstances that were mitigating. He again had been a good man and you knew, in many ways, that he wasn't going to do this again. I gave him a year. He made a strong plea for probation. The government was outraged at the year. And the press was outraged at the year. As the government's press releases up to this point had fanned the flames of the reporter's passions, after that a year seemed like nothing. But the problem was that I felt I had to sentence him on that admission, not anything else that had been alleged. And I wasn't going to let the government try, without a jury, nine-tenths of the case. If they wanted to go to trial, they could have gone to trial. I think the sentence was okay in any event, but those admissions did clearly limit me and I realized that there was a lot I didn't know about the case, but I also accept that as a price of the guilty plea.

The particular view that judges take on real-offense sentencing, as is made evident in the comment cited above, has an enormous impact on the extent to which a defendant may rely on formal charging papers as defining the scope of facts relevant to sentencing. This has importance for the defendant considering whether or not to plead guilty to the charges in an indictment. Judges who restrict themselves to the indictment provide defendants a sense of reliability about the facts that will be taken into account at sentencing. Judges who do not so restrict themselves tend to leave a defendant in a situation of great uncertainty. What we learned is that for most judges, the indictment is neither a full nor a satisfactory source of information. As one judge glibly put it,

You get a preliminary idea of what the government thinks the case is about, but I would say I have been around long enough that I don't start to form any views on sentencing at such an early stage. I think about all the indictment does is set forth the charges and gives me the parameters of the government's case. And I will pick up allegations with regard to, for example, the culpability of the various defendants, the extent to which they profit or profited from the allegedly illegal activities. The indictment, from my point of view, is very much a skeleton, and you only start to put the flesh on the skeleton during the course of the trial, or, if there is a plea of guilty, the flesh is provided in the pre-sentence report.

This perspective, for instance, can legitimate increasing a sentence for tax evasion because the pre-sentence report revealed that the defendant stole from his company the money he failed to report as income, even though there had been no embezzlement charge in the indictment. As one judge stated,

A crime may be charged that, say Mr. X failed to pay taxes on certain expenses that were paid by his company that should have been computed as income but were not. Now when I see in the probation report that Mr. X was misrepresenting himself to the company, I'm going to sentence him for defrauding the company as well as IRS, and I'll do that even where there is no formal charge of that or indication of that in the indictment. I'm interested in the total picture of what was going on, not in the slice selected by the prosecution for inclusion in the indictment. The same goes for the defendant who pleads guilty to $8,000 in tax evasion. When the probation report indicated that there was really $80,000 tax deficit, then I'm sentencing the latter. I'm not concerned about the deal the defendant made to hide the full extent of the deficit.

In regard to the number of counts in the indictment, most of our respondents said that they carried little significance in setting sentence. One judge brought this out when he was asked whether the dropping of counts in the context of a plea bargain had an effect on sentence. The interchange on this issue went like this:

INTERVIEWER: In this case where the corporate executives were stealing from their own company, did the plea of guilty result in a reduced number of charges so that you would be more limited in giving a sentence to those who plead as opposed to those who went to trial?

JUDGE: My recollection is that—I think the answer to that question is no. If he is pleading guilty to a felony charge, which is almost invariably so in this kind of case, even to one count, the court is going to have pretty sobering sentencing options. As you know, the term of years, certain amounts of money, or both. And I don't think that it would be accurate to say that the plea and the consideration for the plea which emerges in these cases has a significant effect upon the court's sentencing powers. Invariably they are charged in a number of counts, and if they plead guilty to only one the judge still has the power to put them in prison. And my reaction would be that consecutive as opposed to concurrent sentences—in a conviction for more than one count—are quite rare to begin with and particularly so I would think in the field of white-collar crime. And if that is true, then it doesn't seem to me that the defendant pleading guilty to one out of four counts, and having the other three dismissed at the time of sentencing, really has such of an effect upon the court's sentencing powers. If the judge wants to send them to prison, he can do so.

Another judge said that where there is only one count there is a technical obstacle to giving a probation period along with a substantial sentence (because the criminal code prevents the imposition of probation in conjunction with a sentence of more than six months' jail time in respect to the same offense) so that occasionally there is an advantage in having two counts in an indictment. But if that particular sentence combination is not sought, then one count usually provides the judge with all the flexibility in sentencing that is needed:

INTERVIEWER: Do the number of counts in the indictment constrain you in any way? Are you attentive to them, do you have to work around them?

JUDGE: In a rare case it constrains you. For instance, if you wanted to give a short sentence and a long period of probation to follow, the statute that governs us says that if you are splitting a single sentence that you cannot impose a combined sentence of probation and a short jail term of more than six months, so if you have one count, you've got to give him six months in jail plus five years' probation or three years' probation. If you got two counts, you can give him one year of jail plus five years' probation; you're without limit except the maximums on the count which are usually much higher than what you're dealing with anyways. Other than that the number of counts don't mean much. A mail fraud scheme can be brought to indictment in five counts, twenty counts or one hundred counts and it can be the same scheme. A guy can have one victim from who he obtains by fraud $5,000 on a phony franchise deal. In the course of bringing this victim along with the scheme, he can write him twenty letters. You could make twenty counts out of the one victim, so it's the number of victims and the amount that ultimately controls the sentencing.

Another judge stated a similar view on this matter, expressing a lack of concern for technical aspects of the charge instrument:

I'm interested in the duration of the crime. Whether this is reflected in the number of counts or not, that question is more basic. Was it a recurrent crime, were there many instances of the behavior? In this securities fraud case we talked about, the brokers were making sales to the public on the basis of false representation. Now the fact that the prosecutor did not charge each sale as a separate count does not prohibit me from taking into account the number of times this was done. Another prosecutor might have charged each sale as one count. The only way to avoid the uneven impact of discrepancy in prosecutorial charging method is to look behind the charging instrument.

Even if they are not accurately reflected in the way the indictment is drawn, facts indicating multiple instances of crime commission and victimization are of concern to judges in every case. The indictment formulated with multiple counts may alert the judge to the possibility of an ongoing or multiple target crime, but it may not distinguish a case in which the prosecutor has inflated the counts for cosmetic purposes from one where multiple counts are truly important.

A major reason why indictments tend not to obtain the status of a formally restrictive legal instrument is the feeling on the part of judges that they are ambiguous and uninformative regarding significant details. For many judges, the indictment simply fails to communicate the essence of the case. This problem can be seen in the following excerpt from an actual indictment that a judge found to be quite inadequate in communicating to him the nature of the offense for which he would have to set sentence. The indictment is essentially limited to defining the offense and therefore the maximum sentence applicablc in the case:

> On or about the 4th day of August . . . the defendant, a resident of _____ and the president and sole owner of _____, a corporation existing and organized under the laws of the State of New York . . . did willfully and knowingly attempt to evade and defeat the income taxes due and owing by said corporation for the fiscal year ending _____, by preparing and causing to be prepared, by signing and causing to be signed, and by mailing and causing to be mailed, . . . a false and fraudulent U.S. Corporation income tax return . . . which was filed with the Internal Revenue Service, wherein he stated that the taxable income of the corporation for the said fiscal year was a net loss of _____ and that no tax was due thereon, whereas, as he then and there well knew, the corporation's taxable income for the said fiscal year was at least _____ and that upon such income a tax of at least _____ was due and owing to the United States of America.

Six other counts are charged, the total fraud lying somewhere between approximately $1,200,000, as charged by the government, and $400,000 as admitted by defense.

Because there was no further detail in the indictment, the judge did not know how the fraud was carried out. Another way of framing the content of the indictment would be to say that the defendant with criminal intent misreported income and thereby with criminal intent failed to pay tax owed to the government. As we will see in what follows, judges are interested in assessing a far richer picture of the offense than this indictment portrays. Going beyond the indictment to other sources of information becomes a primary goal of the sentencing stage of the criminal process.

Assuming that the judge does not feel bound to the formal aspects of the indictment, the extent to which the indictment will constitute the major source of information for making the sentencing decision then depends on how such additional information is brought into the sentencing process. If no other information is brought to the judge, the indictment will naturally stand as the guiding document. This may occur, for instance, when the prosecutor agrees not to bring any background facts to the judge's attention as part of a plea bargain. Such plea bargains are often made in order to restrict information sources so as not to aggravate the seriousness of the crime in the view of the judge. With the judge's agreement a deal may be struck whereby sentence is determined even without a pre-sentence report. Thus the importance of the indictment will vary directly with how much control is exercised over other sources of information. Even a judge who applies strictly the real-offense perspective may not become apprised of the real offense in a case in which the defense attorney is successful in keeping damaging facts out of the arena of decision making.

Pleas and Trials

How do pleas and trials differ as sources of information for the sentencing judge? When researchers think about the difference between pleas and trials they rarely articulate their concerns in terms of the informational content of sentencing decisions. Instead, they concentrate on sentence bargaining, that is, on the existence and magnitude of any discount or reward that may accompany a plea of guilty.[4] What is assumed, if not argued, is that there are systematic differentials in the treatment of offenders based upon their willingness to concede their guilt and thereby save the time, expense, and uncertainty of a formal trial.

Many of the judges with whom we spoke denied that they make explicit or implicit concessions to those who plead guilty. Some, however, acknowledged doing so and defended the practice. They argued that concessions to those who plead guilty encourage and reward cooperation with the state. As one judge explained,

> It is not that the sentence goes up when... [a defendant] goes to trial, but that he gets a slight discount when he pleads guilty. Now, obviously from the defendant's standpoint that distinction doesn't matter.... In my view... if you conceptualize an appropriate sentence for the offender and the offense, you can then make a conscious decision,... so I go up a little bit because he went to trial. ... And I think I am doing the latter. I don't think I have ever said to a guy, well, I thought the right sentence was five years, but he

4. Lynn Mather, *Plea Bargaining or Trial?* (Lexington, Mass.: Lexington Books, 1979).

went to trial so I am going to give him six. But I have consciously thought, well the sentence was whatever—five—but this guy did plead and not only he but the public defender, who has a lot of other defendants, has to get some perception that there is a benefit to be achieved, so I'll give him four.

In chapter 4 we examine in detail the judges' views of the role of the defendant who pleads guilty and cooperates with officials as compared with those who go to trial, but here we are concerned with the way in which the choice of guilty plea or trial affects specifically the flow of information about the case that comes to the judge. Pleas and trials are two very different media of communication. The choice as to whether or not a case should be pled or brought to trial is, from the point of view of the defense, a choice as to how best to manage and present information about the offense and the alleged offender to the judge. Trials give the judge the opportunity to observe the defendant and to hear in great detail the evidence against him. In contrast, where a plea is offered the defendant is before the judge for a short time. Furthermore, prosecution and defense frequently cooperate to present the case in such a way as to convince the judge to accept the plea agreement without making significant additional inquiry about the case. Such an agreement may describe the allegations, provide the evidence that the government believes proves those allegations, and offer a recommendation concerning sentence, thus presenting the judge with all the information necessary for sentencing.

That most judges feel they learn far more about the defendant who goes to trial than about the one who opts for a plea proceeding is exemplified by the following remarks:

> If there has been a trial, I've had exposure at least to the offense and possibly to the offender. . . . At a minimum I will have seen him sitting in the courtroom and you get some impression, maybe not very much and maybe a misleading one, but you just look at a guy for four days and you think you notice some reactions, and he is a presence. That is the minimum. At the maximum, he takes the stand, you may see him for two days of testimony and cross-examination in which you—again it may be misleading, but you feel you come to get a better sense at least of his personality. If it is a plea, you have virtually no sense of either the offense or the offender

until you get the pre-sentence report, the only exception being the day you take the plea. It might be a somewhat elaborate proceeding in which the defendant does say a lot more than just the routine answers to the questions . . . .But I would say that it is probably 5 percent of the cases where enough is said at the plea proceeding to have me feel I got any sense of the man at all.

Another judge put it this way: "What normally happens is that during the trial of the case the judge hears all the gory blood and guts, and he doesn't hear this in a plea."

Though a plea may restrict the amount of information that gets to the judge, the judge is free at the time the plea is entered to conduct an inquiry into the nature of the evidence in the state's possession and to interrogate the defendant to insure that the plea is voluntary and informed, as well as to learn about the defendant's circumstances and motivation. Indeed, the judge may reject the plea in order to force the government to provide more complete explanation of the offense. In one particularly noteworthy case involving an allegation of international bribery by a major corporation, the government had agreed to allow the corporation to plead guilty to one felony count and to pay a modest fine in return for the defendant's agreement to allow the government to examine records that might not otherwise have been subject to subpoena. In the course of examining the plea agreement, the judge in this case noted that there were numerous references to corporate documents in possession of the government that he had not seen. By rejecting the agreement he forced the government to reveal additional information necessary to more fully describe the offense. In this way the judge was able to better satisfy himself that the government could not have fairly charged and obtained a conviction for a more serious offense. Only then did he accept the plea.

While mechanisms exist through which a judge can extract more information than is presented with a plea, the kind of rigorous inquiry pursued in the case described above is clearly exceptional. More often judges must rely on what they are given, knowing that part of the strategy of the guilty plea is to restrict information disclosed to the judge.

Information management is also important in trials, but it is more problematic. The defense does not find it easy to control the details and facts that provide substance and context to the charges. While the defense lawyer may coach his client to develop the presentation of a particular version of facts and personal demeanor, under cross-examination by the prosecution control of facts and demeanor is often greatly weakened. Most of the judges with whom we talked noted that when a case goes to trial the defense takes an "informational risk," a risk that the judge will learn facts about the offense and offender that he would not have known otherwise and that may exert some influence on his sentencing decision.

While responses on this issue varied, most of the judges with whom we spoke indicated that that risk most often redounds against the defendant. The information that comes out at trial leads to greater severity. As one judge explained,

> I think that the information that you get as a result of trials tends to make the sentence harsher than [where there is] a plea. You don't have as much information in front of you of a negative nature from simply the pre-sentence report as you do from having listened to all of the stuff at the trial. And that, I think, tends to make the sentence harsher.

Such harshness results because the judge learns in great detail

> how the thing occurred . . . how deeply involved a person really was, things you often wonder about when you are sentencing. . . . You see the criminal nature of the whole thing or the person. You get a clearer focus than where there's been a plea.

That the effect of a trial, as opposed to a plea, depends on the nature of the offense and offender was expressed by another judge, who disagreed with the proposition that a trial is generally more damaging for the defendant:

> I think that the informational risk . . . generally cuts in a defendant's favor. The guy is much more of a person. . . . When he pleads, it is just a pre-sentence report, it is on paper, you don't know who he is. You can't help but be drawn into a little more of a personal involvement. So that information, I think, more often . . . tends to help the guy. Sometimes it hurts. Sometimes some aspects of him come through that I think make him seem a less meritorious person than if he had just pled guilty and appeared for sentencing. But I think more often than not the mitigating factors come through. He

appears more the victim of circumstance, . . . the victim of a tough, down-on-his-luck situation. He doesn't seem like such a bad guy. What I suspect happens, and I am not sure of this, is that I get that fuller information and maybe become a little more sympathetic, and then I kind of weigh it all. So I am not sure going to trial the guy is always the worse off.

The difference between pleas and trials as sources of information appears to be particularly important in white-collar cases. In those cases the character of the defendant, his motivation, and his circumstances are often of central importance in establishing the existence of fraudulent intent. Typically, white-collar defense strategy seeks to portray the defendant as an innocent victim of circumstance. Several judges noted that trials serve to break through the facade that the defense tries to present by exposing avarice as the primary motivation for the offense. Furthermore, white-collar cases often raise complex issues of fact, of multiple, shared, and relative culpability, and questions about the precise nature and duration of the alleged offense. The utility of the trial in exposing and unraveling complex factual situations is aptly described by a judge who had to make a sentencing decision in a case involving the falsification of financial records in an investment banking business:

> In the case that I am talking about there was a three- or four-week trial. It was very thorough. I saw the witnesses; I saw the defendant on direct examination and on cross-examination . . . I heard tremendous detail about the background and the surrounding circumstances, the details that constituted the crime and a kind of attempt to cover it up afterwards. . . .
>
> There were conflicts in the evidence about exactly what happened. Now a big part of what happened related to exactly who did what in connection with falsifying the statements. There were certain activities that involved the literal production of some accounting records so that accountants could see them. Writing out false accounting records—and who was responsible for doing that, for directing that it be done? How long did this go on? At what time did certain people begin to have some qualms and one of them ultimately told the accountants about the problem? It was a very complex story. And in it . . . you knew where the conflicts were and where the things were that were clear, but all in all you knew a lot

of evidence relating to precisely what the deeds were, how culpable they were. . . . I had the whole picture spelled out to me . . . by three or four witnesses . . . to what the defendant did to cause this, what did he say, how well did he signal that . . . he was giving the direction. . . . You know, how crafty was the scheme. . . . Testimony in this case went back two years before the events in question. . . . If he had come in and . . . said, "Your Honor, I plead guilty to one count of conspiracy," there would be an admission of guilt, but I wouldn't know how the crime had been committed, the exact extent of his knowledge, how he insulated himself from doing the dirty work. . . . I could go on and on with details that put meat on the bones of a so-called admission of crime.

The damage caused by going to trial is compounded when the defendant takes the stand and is perceived to be lying or testifying disingenuously. We found considerable evidence that judges weigh the truthfulness of testimony given by the defendant heavily in their sentencing decisions. While most judges deny that they impose an additional sentence for unproved perjury, they argue that they legitimately seek to assess the defendant's character in deciding among alternative sentences and that lying on the stand is one indication of character. Discussing the case of a minister involved in an auto sales fraud, one judge explained,

The sentencing judge has a prime desire and need to know that defendant as well as he can, and one of the ways you come to know him is by his performance on the witness stand. . . . [Y]ou get a reading of the kind of person he is, and in this instance, I had a man of the cloth who doesn't mind sitting on the witness chair utilizing his appearance, place, position, and every other such thing, to gain favor with the jury. He was artful in his performance, but he didn't fool the jury. . . . [H]e categorically denied certain occurrences, the evidence to the contrary being overwhelmingly against him. I thought he was a fool . . . to do that, but he was taking his only way out.

Another judge described the defendant in a franchise fraud:

He made a bad mistake. He testified in his own behalf and his testimony at the trial was false. He took the stand and accused several of his subordinates of misconduct, cheating him, cheating the franchisers. . . . I was pretty indignant at the end of the trial. I thought that he had started out by defrauding his franchisers and then he came in and tried to defraud the jury as well.

In all of these cases the amount and quality of information available to the sentencing judge after a trial is significantly different from that after a guilty plea. Some of that information is relatively concrete, some of it merely impressionistic. Its effect is clearly to broaden the basis of decision at sentencing by expanding the judge's understanding of the offense and offender.

The Pre-Sentence Report

The core of the informational network operative in sentencing decisions, at least in the federal courts, is the pre-sentence report.[5] For the vast majority of criminal cases this report is prepared by the probation department serving each federal court. It contains a broad range of facts about the defendant's life, his family, education, occupational history, physical and mental disorders, financial situation, and reputation. In addition, it may contain a detailed description of the offense and of prior arrests and convictions. It provides information about sentence severity in the form of a recommendation made for sentence by the probation officer and from statistics of district or national sentencing patterns. Finally, it contains an evaluative summary prepared by the probation officer. The summary is based upon interviews with the defendant and sometimes his lawyer, the prosecutor, relevant law enforcement agencies, friends, family, and associates of the defendant, as well as a review of documents or records of educational and financial institutions.[6] In this sense, the pre-sentence reports serve to help individualize the sentencing process by providing the judge with an in-depth portrait and characterization of each offender. Where, as in the vast majority of cases, there is no trial the report often substitutes for the trial itself as a mechanism through which facts are found in a criminal case. In those cases, the report provides the sentencing judge with his only knowledge of the offense and the defendant, other than the minimal facts necessary to support the acceptance of a guilty plea.[7]

5. Robert Dawson, *Sentencing* (Boston: Little, Brown, 1969), pp. 24–41.

6. David Gronewold, "Presentence Investigation Practices in the Federal Probation System," 22 *Federal Probation* 27 (1958); S. A. Fennell and W. H. Hall, "Due Process at Sentencing," 93 *Harvard Law Review* 1613 (1980).

7. Fennell and Hall, "Due Process at Sentencing," 1627; see also note, "Pro-

Moreover, much of the information contained in the pre-sentence report concerning the defendant's personal background is not likely to come out even in cases in which there are trials. As a result, the pre-sentence report is a primary source of information about the offender.

Pre-sentence reports are a relatively new source of information for the sentencing judge. Their origins can be traced to the Federal Probation Act of 1925. That act authorized release on probation as a criminal penalty and permitted the establishment of probation offices, the primary function of which was to be the supervision of offenders placed on probation.[8] During the early part of the twentieth century the rehabilitative ideal became the dominant ideology of criminal punishment in the United States.[9] It treats crime as if it were a symptom of illness and places in the hands of law enforcement officials the responsibility for diagnosis and treatment.

The rehabilitative ideal is relevant to our consideration of sentencing as an information-gathering process because it emphasizes the importance of both the quantity and quality of information available to the judge about the individual offender. If the judge's job is to classify the offender as to character, motivation, needs, then background information is critical to that task.[10] The rehabilitative ideal emphasizes the need to make the fullest possible inquiry into the person committing the criminal act. As Justice Black wrote in describing the task of the judge under that model,

---

cedural Due Process at Judicial Sentencing for Felony," 81 *Harvard Law Review* 821 (1968).

8. As the need for information became more widely acknowledged, judges began to turn to the probation department as the tool for obtaining it. The relationship between judges and probation officers was standardized in 1946 by the enactment of Rule 32(L) (I) of the Federal Rules of Criminal Procedure, which required that probation officers prepare pre-sentence reports on all criminal defendants unless specifically directed not to by the court. That rule provides that those reports "shall contain any prior criminal record of the defendant and such information about this character, his financial condition and the circumstances affecting his behavior as may be helpful in imposing sentence." At present the basic structure of the pre-sentence report is pretty well standardized throughout the federal court system, although there is some district-by-district variation in its precise content.

9. Francis Allen, *The Borderland of Criminal Justice* (Chicago: University of Chicago Press, 1964).

10. John Coffee, "The Future of Sentencing Reform," 73 *Michigan Law Review* (1975) 1361.

His task within fixed statutory or constitutional limits is to determine the type and extent of punishment after the issue of guilt has been determined. Highly relevant—if not essential—to his selection of an appropriate sentence is the possession of the fullest information concerning the defendant's life and characteristics. And modern concepts individualizing punishment have made it all the more necessary that a sentencing judge not be denied an opportunity to obtain pertinent information by a requirement of rigid adherence to restrictive rules of evidence.[11]

The use of pre-sentence reports has engendered a great deal of critical commentary. Some worry about reliance on background information, for example, school records, that is often far removed in time from the current situation of the offender.[12] Others question the reliability and accuracy of the testimonial evidence that is gathered and the adequacy of attempts at verification.[13] They cite examples of errors in pre-sentence reports that led to substantially greater punishment than would otherwise have been justified.[14] This concern about accuracy is an indicator of the probation report's central role in bringing information to the judge.[15]

11. Williams v. New York, 337 U.S. 241 (1948). Similarly, a former federal district judge wrote nearly forty years ago, "The knowledge of the life of a man, his background and his family, is the only proper basis for the determination as to his treatment. The sentencing judge in the federal court has the tools with which to acquire that information. Failure to make full use of those tools cannot be justified." Lewis Schwellenbach, "Information versus Intuition in the Imposition of Sentence," 27 *Journal of the American Judicature Society* 52 (1943).

12. Coffee, "The Future of Sentencing Reform," 1395; see also Dawson, *Sentencing*.

13. Robert Carter and Leslie Wilkins, "Some Factors in Sentencing Policy," 58 *Journal of Criminal Law* 503 (1967); Coffee, "The Future of Sentencing Reform"; Donald Katkin, "Presentence Reports," 55 *Minnesota Law Review* 15 (1970); William Campbell, "Delays in Criminal Cases," 55 *Federal Rules Decisions* 229 (1972); Mempa v. Rhau, 389 U.S. 128 (1967); U.S. v. Woody, 567 F. 2d 1353 (1978); U.S. v. Needles, 472 F. 2d 652 (1973); Fennell and Hall, "Due Process at Sentencing," 1634.

14. In one case, U.S. v. Weston, 448 F. 2d 626 (1971), the inclusion of an uncorroborated and erroneous charge that the defendant was a major drug supplier caused the sentencing judge to abandon his announced intention of imposing a five-year prison term and to impose, instead, a maximum twenty-year sentence.

15. Concerns about the accuracy and reliability of information in the pre-sentence report have been regularly reflected in commentaries calling for the imposition of due process requirements during sentencing and the disclosure of pre-sentence reports to the defense (see Katkin, "Presentence Reports," Campbell, "Delays in

When a defendant pleads guilty to an ambiguous charge the pre-sentence report will have critical detail about the nature of the offense as well as about the background and character of the offender. The following excerpt from the pre-sentence report in the case of tax fraud cited earlier in this chapter shows the manner in which that report can significantly expand a judge's understanding of the true conduct of the defendant:

> IRS agents have determined that the defendant's unreported income for the stores... from ____1976 through ____1979 amounted to [over $1 million].... According to these figures the defendant owes additional corporate taxes and penalties... In addition the defendant owes back taxes and penalties on his personal tax returns... amounting to [over $1 million].
>
> This ____-year-old defendant pleaded guilty to evading ____ in corporate taxes for the fiscal year ending April 30, ____. However, the total amount of personal and corporate taxes he had avoided is substantial. According to the records of the Internal Revenue Service, this defendant withheld large amounts of cash sales from deposits to the corporate accounts of four of his... stores. He diverted the currency to his safe deposit boxes, which he controlled, and kept this information from his accountants.

Criminal Cases," and Coffee, "The Future of Sentencing Reform"). While the courts have resisted the imposition of the full range of due process rights at sentencing, they have recognized the right to counsel as an essential postdisposition right (Mempa v. Rhau, 389 U.S. 128 [1967]). Moreover, some court decisions explicitly recognize a defendant's right to be sentenced on the basis of accurate and reliable information and to have the opportunity to scrutinize and challenge information contained in the pre-sentence report. (See Townsend v. Burke, 334 U.S. 736 [1947], in which the court invalidated the conviction of a defendant who was sentenced on patently inaccurate information in the pre-sentence report that was used by the trial judge in setting sentence; see also, for example, U.S. v. Woody, 567 F.2d 1353 [1978], and U.S. v. Needles, 472 F.2d 652 [1973]). The constitutionality of the use of pre-sentence reports in state criminal proceedings was established in Williams v. New York, 337 U.S. 241 (1949) in an opinion written by Justice Black.

In 1975, the Supreme Court approved and Congress adopted an amendment to the Federal Rules of Criminal Procedure requiring disclosure of the factual sections of the pre-sentence report. The rule does not require disclosure of the probation officer's recommendation or of information obtained under a promise of confidentiality along with information that in the opinion of the judge might result in harm to the defendant or to others (Fennell and Hall, "Due Process at Sentencing," 1634).

When IRS agents asked to examine these books the defendant instructed an employee to assist him in the fabrication of the sales figures for two of his stores.

This is the case of an individual who started a small business and through diligence and effort saw it grow and prosper. He apparently worked long hours and continues to do so and he has reached the point where he now owns seven . . . stores and a service corporation. However, somewhere along the line he became overcome by greed and decided to keep two sets of books, one for tax purposes and the other to reflect the true financial activities of his business . . . . He has not paid any of his back taxes and he claims that his personal tax returns and corporate net worth are matters which are pending final resolution with the IRS. The defendant's explanation as to why he committed the instant offense, that is, that he exercised bad judgment, is certainly an understatement considering the dishonest pattern that the defendant has established and the amount of money involved.

Given the importance of the pre-sentence report and the controversies surrounding its disclosure and use, we were not surprised to find a wide variety of attitudes about the pre-sentence report among the judges whom we interviewed. Some judges believe that the probation officer is a neutral, impartial source of information, perhaps the only neutral and impartial source available to them. As stated by one judge,

> Sure. How else does a judge get information? If he doesn't get it there he very seldom gets it because otherwise he is getting only stories which will come from allocution, from the defendant himself, or his counsel. We know that has to be by its nature advocacy. The probation officer has no axe to grind.

Others believe that the probation officer tailors the report to his perception of what will influence the judge, and that the routinization of the information typically found in the report discourages probation officers from seeking and providing unusual, but pertinent, sources of information. As one judge said,

> Well, as you know, you get from the probation department the pre-sentence report. . . . I think . . . that after a little while what they do is they try to pattern that . . . pre-sentence report for what you

want to read. They, in other words, gauge what sort of individual you are and are more inclined to write something that they think would be acceptable to you.

And still others have an even more skeptical attitude about these reports:

> The pre-sentence report is, for me, the beginning of the inquiry, not the end. It rarely answers all of my questions. Indeed, it generally raises as many questions as it answers. Pre-sentence reports frequently contain factual errors, errors which often are not caught. Too many judges are too reliant on pre-sentence reports; they are easily abused. For me they are simply one aid to my decision. They shouldn't provide the decision ready-made and wrapped up.

Given the breadth and scope of information provided in the report, it is not surprising that judges display differential interest in and sensitivity to different parts of it. Here are two judges who appear to use of the pre-sentence report in quite different ways:

> I don't consider relevant what the siblings are doing and things like that. I do consider relevant the kind of childhood he had, the family he came from, the opportunities he had in life, the record he has, the intelligence he has or doesn't have . . . Their criminal record is most important.

> I look at the whole thing. I look at, number one, the official version of the offense, the defendant's version, and I attempt to reach some kind of conclusion as to how candid I really think the defendant is in regard to his version . . . I'm interested in his record of employment. I'm very much interested in the prior offenses. I'm less interested in family background . . .

In addition to facts about the offense and offender, one of the most important pieces of information presented is the probation officer's recommended sentence. The recommendation provided by the probation officer may be for a specific sentence, for example, incarceration for five years, or simply a statement as to whether incarceration or probation seems appropriate. Some judges express doubt about the utility of those recommendations, and they are reluctant to transfer their sentencing responsibility to the probation department. They believe that having the facts is important, but that the translation of them into a specific sentence is the exclusive province of the judge. A recommendation on this issue is thus inappropriate. Others, however, see the probation officer's recommendation as critical. They believe that the probation officer is a "professional sentencer" who has both a broad view of a range of cases and sentences and in-depth, detailed knowledge of the particular case for which a recommendation is made. Indeed, some judges seem so deferential to the recommendation that they rarely deviate from it:

> I find that when I receive a pre-sentence report, I always look at the end . . . first to see what the probation department recommends. I am always relieved when they recommend probation because nobody likes to impose a prison sentence and it is swimming upstream for a judge to impose a lesser sentence than the probation department recommends.

Whatever attitudes judges hold about the impartiality or completeness of information transmitted by the probation department, it is apparent that all judges rely on at least part of the pre-sentence report for learning what they consider to be relevant facts about the defendant's background.

Sentencing Memoranda

After the disposition and before the sentence is entered, the judge may invite or accept memoranda from the prosecution and/or defense in which they present their view of the case and their ideas about an appropriate sentence. Sometimes these memoranda are designed to respond to, challenge, or clarify material presented in the pre-sentence report. Sometimes they present new or additional information that would not have been admissible during the dispositional phase. In many instances, this places the judge in the position of having to evaluate facts not subject to rebuttal or refutation and of having to relate those facts to the formal version in an indictment or to a narrower version of facts that came out in a trial or in a pre-sentence report.

In examining the files of white-collar cases prosecuted during the research period, we found many cases in which the sentencing memoranda were long and detailed documents. Typically they presented

extensive statements of facts that bore on the nature of the offense—
for instance, what was the true extent of the damage caused, how
many persons were involved, what was its duration, any special circumstances; and on the nature of the offender—for instance, what
motivated the defendant, whether the defendant gained personally,
how the defendant will be affected personally by particular sanctions.

In many respects, the sentencing memoranda operate as both evi-
dentiary device and closing legal arguments. They are used to bring
new information to the judge as well as to interpret the entire range
of information available about a case. Defense attorneys may also use
these memoranda to challenge inaccuracies in the pre-sentence reports. In all instances they have the effect of intensifying the degree
of adversariness at sentencing. Many judges believe that defense attorneys miss a critical opportunity to have an influence on sentencing
when they fail to prepare a sentencing memorandum or when their
preparation is inadequate, though other judges expressed the view
that attorneys prepare these documents mainly to impress their clients,
not judges.

As an example of how a defense attorney will use a sentencing
memorandum, consider these edited selections from a ten-page letter
and forty-page memorandum prepared by attorneys in a case of tax
fraud (the same case for which edited excerpts of the indictment and
pre-sentence report were presented above). In the first excerpt, we
see the defense attorney attempt to correct mistakes or misimpressions
created, it was argued, by faulty work on the part of the probation
officer who prepared the pre-sentence report.

We are attorneys for _____, who is scheduled to be sentenced on
_____. On _____ Mr. _____ waived indictment and _____ entered a
plea of guilty to Count One . . . charging him with corporate income
tax evasion (26 U.S.C.§ 7201). This letter is submitted to apprise
the Court of certain material errors and misleading information
attributed to the Internal Revenue Service, and contained in the
pre- sentence report submitted by the Probation Department in
regard to Mr. _____.

By relying on inaccurate and speculative information developed
by the Internal Revenue Service during its investigation in this case,
the pre-sentence report mistakenly and unjustifiably concludes that
Mr. _____, "overcome by greed", consciously embarked on a massive

tax fraud scheme . . . . This presentation of the facts does not comport with the truth.

Without describing or identifying any supporting evidence, the pre-sentence report asserts that ___had total "verified" unreported income in the amount of ___.

In calculating taxable income for the corporations in question, the agents failed to reduce gross receipts by the amount of cost of goods sold and by the amount of certain deductible business expenses actually incurred or properly accruable.

It is most unfortunate that the errors made by the Service in calculating corporate taxable income . . . have now re-emerged to distort the pre-sentence report offered to the Court for reliance in rendering judgment.

The second excerpt focuses on that part of the sentencing memorandum that attempts to establish the high moral quality of the defendant, implying that the crime to which he pled guilty was a single deviation in an otherwise exemplary career. First come testimonials from the defendant's son and his wife, second, a recitation of the defendant's high standing as evidenced by statements of friends and associates, and third, a statement of factors weighing against imposition of a prison sentence. From the defendant's son:

> Ever since I was little my father and I have had a very special relationship. He is always there for me when I need him. If I need his advice he always tries to help me with it. Even if he's at work. I feel that if I could call him with a problem he'll always be more than happy to help me with it. He has helped all of his kids with all different types of problems. We all need him very much!

And from his wife:

> To have my husband sent to prison will be more than I could [bear]. It will be the last straw my emotions could possibly take . . . . I have been stretched to the limits of human endurance. I pray you find it in your judgment to show kindness and mercy.

About the defendant's standing in the community:

> One of the strongest arguments in favor of leniency for _____ is the picture which emerges from the comments of a representative group of people who have known and observed him for years, and

whose judgment is reliable and experienced. Their words on his behalf are compelling evidence of . . . inherent decency, compassion and commitment to charity, and the admiration, respect, warmth and love that so many people have for him. Mindful of the need for brevity, a careful selection has been given the Court of the views of a cross-section of the community.

The themes reported in letter after letter are Mr. ____'s kindness, generosity, and thoughtfulness of others.

Horace . . . writes that he has "little difficulty extolling the virtues of this man. ____ is one of the community's most respected members for his consistent display of fine character and generosity to any worthwhile endeavor"

The warmth felt for ____ by his friends and associates perhaps is best expressed by his employees, with whom he comes into daily contact:

"How does one begin to describe the warmth, sincerity and decency of ____ in a humane way. When other employers would have ignored their employee's hardship due to illness, Mr. ____ unselfishly provided them with some financial remuneration they received while working. Again let me say that Mr. ____ is the most compassionate human being that I have ever known."

The memorandum concludes in part:

In this case, numerous undisputed factors weigh heavily against the imposition of a sentence of imprisonment. The sole blot on Mr. ____'s record is his present conviction. Mr. ____, by his plea, has acknowledged his wrongdoing and has spared the Court and the Government the burden and expense of a trial. Although he has never before been convicted of any offense, this single conviction, which has already been widely reported in the press, will irretrievably tarnish Mr. ____'s reputation in the community for honesty and integrity, which he has enjoyed until the present. Mr. ____ and his family have already suffered greatly from the shame, humiliation and agonized uncertainty which have attended this criminal investigation and prosecution. Mr. ____ has already paid ____ to the IRS in payment of taxes, interest and penalties to be assessed and stands ready to make substantial additional payments . . . . The publicity resulting from Mr. ____'s plea of guilty, and knowledge of his guilty plea throughout the community have already benefited society by deterring others who may be tempted to commit similar violations of the law.

Sentencing memoranda are clearly useful in providing judges with information about the defendant's character and may be useful in identifying characteristics of the offense, though the sentencing memorandum in the instant case emphasized more the character of the offender than the offense.

In many cases, the sentencing memoranda go beyond the pre-sentence reports in helping the judge to understand the case. In cases of substantive complexity, the offense of conviction often leaves open questions about the nature of the defendant's behavior. This tends to be true in fraud cases in which the offense section is unusually ambiguous in defining the behavior it encompasses:

> Where [a sentencing memorandum] is of particular value to me would be where it is a complicated case, and where there are considerations that perhaps the probation department in preparing its pre-sentence report may not be fully competent. For example, we have some very fine people in the probation department, but they may not know mutual funds, they may not know banking operations, and so I think in the white-collar area sentencing memoranda would be particularly good.

In this situation, the defense and prosecution sentencing memoranda are quickly becoming an important addition to the pre-sentence investigation report. This is so in part because the reporting mode of the pre-sentence report, which was originally developed primarily for violent crime and street crime and in which the major force of inquiry was the susceptibility of the defendant to rehabilitation, is not fitted well to the questions asked by judges in white-collar cases. And when defendants have substantial resources to invest in attorneys' fees, the preparation of a detailed statement of facts and legal arguments in a written document may have an important impact on the nature of the sentencing hearing.

Allocution

At the time of sentencing, defendants are provided an opportunity to make a statement presenting information that is relevant to the judge's decision. This is called the allocution, and it comes late in the process, after the judge has received and had time to absorb all other sources of information. Nevertheless, it may be useful, especially in cases disposed through a guilty plea, in that it allows the judge to get an impression of the defendant who has not communicated directly with the judge other than by making the formal statements necessary to complete the guilty plea procedure. Here the defendant can attempt to explain his role in the crime and give the judge an opportunity to assess the overall moral character of the person, an issue, as we shall see more in chapter 4, that often has an impact on how a judge determines the sentence. Though defense attorneys influence the way in which a defendant handles the allocution, judges feel that in their reading of it they can often pick up a sign of remorsefulness, or lack thereof, or get a better understanding of why the defendant did what he did.

The sentencing decision emerges at the end of a long process of information acquisition and interpretation. The single most important document in the routine case is the pre-sentence investigation report. But white-collar cases are often not treated routinely at sentencing. The complex nature of the offense and the high level of adversariness that often characterizes the sentencing process result in a broader and more intensive assessment of the factual elements of the case. Within this process, judges are not merely passive recipients of information, they are active interpreters. They must construct a portrait of the defendant as a prerequisite to deciding what sentence to mete out.

The factors that feed into that decision are many, but most of them relate to one or another of three fundamental concerns: the amount of harm caused by the offense, the blameworthiness of the offender, and the consequence of the sanction to be imposed.

■ 3

Assessing the Offense: Harm and Seriousness

Harm is harm and should be paid for. —Pollock and Maitland, History of English Law

When judges discuss why one defendant is given a longer sentence than another, they typically begin that discussion with an assessment of the seriousness of the case. Judges seek to cull from the information available to them a picture of what was done, to whom, in what ways, and also a picture of the circumstances, history, and behavior of the offender. A case for them is the combination of an offender and an offense, and it is not always clear when and how they separate offense and offender. Indeed, for some, if an offense is more serious, its perpetrator is therefore more culpable; the two qualities are thus inextricably linked. But for most judges, commentary is devoted separately to the nature of the offense itself and to the nature of the defendant.

We have tried to maintain that distinction, though we recognize a certain artificiality in the process. We begin our consideration of the way judges assess the seriousness of white-collar crime with those attributes that go most directly to the nature of the offense and close with one important indicator of the severity of the offense, the presence or absence of the violation of trust, a point at which the distinction between offense and offender is most difficult to sustain. In chapter 4, we deal with the other major component of the seriousness of a case, namely, the blameworthiness of the defendant.

It is clear from our interviews that the key element in the assessment of the offense is an assessment of harm done. Judges say harm is central to the determination of the gravity of the offense. While some judges, in fact, use the term *gravity*, others speak about the *severity* of the offense. Still others refer to how *damaging* the offense is. Furthermore, the detailed and specific meaning they give to these words, whichever they use, varies from judge to judge. But if asked to explain a particular sentence, all would agree with one judge who said, "You have to remember that fundamentally a crime is a social harm. You look to see what is the social harm, and usually the extent of social harm is determined by the number of people who are hurt, and the pervasiveness of the crime."

Harm as a Core Legal Norm

In giving harm caused by an offense a prominent place in their thinking, judges are in effect reaching back through centuries of formal law to an understanding about the nature of criminal conduct that infuses our legal thinking. The idea that harm should be a prerequisite to and at the same time a standard for determining the length of the sentence is a recurring theme in Anglo-American jurisprudence. A typical statement of the relationship of punishment and harm is found in Stephen's *History of the Criminal Law of England*. He defined harm as the very object of the criminal law: "In different ages of the world injuries to individuals, to God, to the gods, or to the community, have been treated as crimes, but I think that in all cases the idea of crime has involved the idea of some definite, gross, undeniable injury to some one."[1]

While what constitutes harm or injury certainly varies with culture and over time, the occurrence of an event or action identified as harmful is necessary to justify punishment. In the earliest societies, "the few crimes which were considered a danger to the public and, *hence*, punished by the whole local group, were those which exposed the group to outside dangers from spiritual or human enemies" (emphasis added).[2] So clear is the association of harm and punishment in our current legal culture that critics argue that so-called victimless crimes (for example, prostitution) are unfit for legal sanction because no real harm has been done to others.

Long before the term *victimless crime* came into use, the same libertarian motive brought John Stuart Mill in his landmark essay *On Liberty* to claim that "the only purpose for which power can be rightfully exercised over any member of a civilised community, against his

1. Sir James Fitzjames Stephen, *A History of the Criminal Law of England* (London: Macmillan, 1883), 2:78.
2. Harry Elmer Barnes, *The Story of Punishment: A Record of Man's Inhumanity to Man* (Boston: Stratford, 1930), 42.

will, is to prevent harm to others."[3] In detailing his defense of individual liberty, Mill defined the role of punishment in a clear and distinct manner:

> Though doing no wrong to any one, a person may so act to compel us to judge him.... We [then] have a right,... to act upon our unfavourable opinion.... We are not bound, for example, to seek his society;... [however] Acts injurious of others require a totally different treatment... —these are fit objects of moral reprobation, and, in grave cases, of moral retribution and punishment.[4]

Mill's writings even today have a central place in the ongoing debate about how the criminal law should define harm.[5] Herbert Packer, for example, draws directly on Mill to assert that "harm to others" must be a "limiting criteri[on] for invocation of the criminal sanction."[6]

The first significance of harm in Anglo-American jurisprudence is, then, as a prerequisite to the criminal sanction. The second significance of harm—one no less important to judges—is as a measure of the seriousness of the offense and therefore as a standard for determining the severity of the sentence that will be meted out.

Perhaps the earliest statement that punishment should be measured by harm done is the *Lex talionis*, which contains the widely known principle "An eye for an eye, a tooth for a tooth."[7] The ancient Romans also used harm to help rank the seriousness of crimes. For

3. *On Liberty and Considerations on Representative Government* (Oxford: Basil Blackwell, 1946), 8.

4. Ibid.

5. In a public controversy over the recommendation for law reform submitted in England in the Wolfenden Report in 1957 Hart cites Mill in support of the committee's recommendation to decriminalize homosexuality, while Devlin cites Mill in support of the proposition that the criminal law should properly be used to enforce moral standards. See H. L. A. Hart, *Law, Liberty and Morality* (New York: Random House, 1966), and Patrick Devlin, *Enforcement of Morals* (Oxford: Oxford University Press, 1965), esp. chap. 5.

6. *The Limits of the Criminal Sanction* (Stanford: Stanford University Press, 1968), 267.

7. "If he strike, and hurt a woman with child, so that her fruit depart from her, and yet no mischief follow: he shall be surely punished, according as the woman's husband will lay upon him; and he shall pay as the judges determine. / And if any mischief follow, then thou shalt give life for life, / eye for eye, tooth for tooth, hand for hand, foot for foot, / burning for burning, wound for wound, stripe for stripe." Exodus, 21:22–23.

example, the *Institutes* of Justinian, a codification of much of Roman law from around A.D. 533, provided greater penalties for assaults in which a person was beaten with a club than for assaults without a weapon.[8]

In English law, the historical literature is quite unanimous on at least one point: until the early eighteenth century torture and capital punishment were systematic and widespread. Describing English penal law, the legal historian Stephen noted, "[T]he early criminal law was extremely severe.... In the case of persons who could not read, all felonies, including manslaughter, every kind of theft above the value of a shilling, and all robbery were capital crimes."[9] And in Italy, the intellectual home of the early reform movement in penology, "there was scarcely an act in the possible category of crimes that was not then punishable by death."[10] It was this extreme severity of punishments that compelled the great eighteenth-century reformers to act. On the Continent and in England, their thinking spurred the change that gave us what are still fundamental precepts about the relationship of harm and punishment.

In Italy, Cesare Beccaria, probably the most important theorist of penal reform of that age, found the greatest injustice in the then large disproportion between punishments and crimes. As he saw it, there was insufficient distinction in the law between such different crimes as theft and murder in as much as both could result in death. His small pamphlet *Crimes and Punishments*, which attacked the "cruelty" of the criminal law, was to be swooped up in Europe and England, and it became the principal force in penal reform.[11]

It was Beccaria who spread the idea, derivative of a general theory of utility, that "the punishment should fit the crime." In the context of the truly outlandish severity of criminal law at that time, his was a revolutionary idea. He believed punishments had to be changed, and by this he meant reduced, to reflect more precisely the gravity of those particular crimes that would carry the death penalty. For Beccaria—

8. *Institutes of Justinian*, book IV, title IV, in Douglas George Cracknell, *Roman Law* (London: Butterworth, 1964).
9. Stephen, *History of Criminal Law*, 1:466–67.
10. James Anson Farrer, *Crimes and Punishments, Including a New Translation of Beccaria's "Dei delittie e delle pene"* (London: Chatto and Windus, 1880), 10.
11. Coleman Phillipson, *Three Criminal Law Reformers: Beccaria, Bentham, Romilly* (London: J. M. Dent, 1923).

this is a hallmark in his theory of punishment—taking such a step
meant adjusting the punishment to correlate with the harm done to
society:

> Not only is it the general interest that crimes should not be com-
> mitted, but that they should be rare in proportion to the evils they
> cause to society. The more opposed therefore that crimes are to the
> public welfare, ... the stronger should be the repellant obstacles.
> This principle accordingly establishes the necessity of a certain pro-
> portion between crimes and punishments.[12]

It is true that Beccaria's theory of punishment required "proof"
that the persons held out for punishment had actually done what they
were accused of doing. In this sense a definite requirement of blameworthiness exists as a prerequisite for punishment. But exactly what
kind of mental state is required in order that the so-called wrongdoer
be punished is left ambiguous. In distinct contrast, great emphasis is
put on adjusting the punishment to the measure of harm caused to
society. Said Beccaria,

> We have seen that the true measure of crimes is the injury done to
> society. This is one of those palpable truths which, however little
> dependent on quadrants or telescopes for their discovery, and fully
> within the reach of any ordinary intelligence, are yet, by marvellous
> combination of circumstances, only recognized clearly and firmly
> by some few thinkers, belonging to every nationality and to every
> age. . . .
>
> They who have thought that the criminal's intention was the true
> measure of crimes were in the wrong. For the intention depends on
> the actual impression of things on a man and his precedent mental
> disposition, things which vary in all men and in each man, according
> to the very rapid succession of his ideas, his passions, and his cir-
> cumstances. It would, therefore, be necessary to form not only a
> particular code for each citizen, but a fresh law for each crime.
> Sometimes with the best intentions men do the greatest evil to
> society; and sometimes with the very worst they do it the greatest
> good. [Beccaria, as cited in Farrer, *Crimes and Punishments*, pp.
> 199–200]

12. Farrer, *Crimes and Punishments*, 196.

Beccaria's theories seeped deeply into the English common law and influenced many legal scholars.[13] Blackstone, a jurist of singular authority in shaping American as well as English common law, relies heavily on Beccaria in his dissertation on the criminal law, taking a similar view, for instance, of the crimes to which capital punishment should be applied: "[S]o dreadful a list, instead of diminishing, increases the number of offenders."[14]

In his *Commentaries on the Laws of England* (1765–69) Blackstone espoused his view on punishment this way: "for the greater and more exalted the object of an injury is, the more care should be taken to prevent that injury, and of course under this aggravation the punishment should be more severe."[15] Blackstone articulated in England what Beccaria had brought to Europe:

> It is . . . absurd and impolitic to apply the same punishment to crimes of different malignity. . . . It is a kind of quackery in government, and argues a want of solid skill, to apply the same universal remedy, the *ultimum supplicium* (the severest or capital punishment), to every case of difficulty. . . . It has therefore been ingeniously proposed that in every state a scale of crimes should be formed, with a corresponding scale of punishments, descending from the greatest to the least.[16]

Fitting the punishment to social ends meant designing, in Blackstone's words, a "scale" of punishments for a "scale" of crimes.

These principles came into American legal culture through two main paths. First, in enacting the Eighth Amendment to the Constitution, the Framers used the language of the English Bill of Rights,[17] which

13. Farrer, an English legal scholar, was able to write in 1880, "Whatever improvement our penal laws have undergone in the last hundred years is due primarily to Beccaria, and to an extent that has not always been recognized. . . . [T]here is no English writer of that day who, in treating of the criminal law, does not refer to Beccaria" (ibid., 46). Bentham and Blackstone were heavily influenced by Beccaria. It has been said that Bentham saw Beccaria as his "master" (Phillipson, *Three Criminal Law Reformers*, 92).

14. Sir William Blackstone, *Commentaries on the Laws of England*, book IV, sec. 18, p. 19, ed. William Carey Jones (San Francisco: Bancroft-Whitney 1916), 2173.

15. Ibid., book IV, sec. 13, p. 15, 2168.

16. Ibid., 2168–69.

17. See reference in United States v. Helm, 463 U.S. 277.

read, "excessive Baile ought not to be required nor excessive Fines imposed nor cruell and unusuall Punishments inflicted."[18] In adopting this language the Framers made the English common law principle of proportionality a fundamental concept of American justice. Indeed, a leading case dealing with the Eighth Amendment, *Weems v. United States*,[19] held that "it is a precept of justice that punishment for crime should be graduated and proportioned to offense."[20] And since *Weems* the Court has used English sources of law to guide its interpretation of the Eighth Amendment.[21]

The second path was through legislative grading of crimes and penalties on the basis of harm done. Legislative grading means classification of crimes, for the purpose of setting penalties, into groups indicating a judgment about relative severity.

Systems for classifying crimes, whether in England or the United States, have generally relied on two distinctions.[22] One focuses on the size of the harm, the other on the object or interest injured by the crime.[23] As an example of how American penal law developed by

18. Ibid.

19. 217 U.S. 349, 30 S. Ct. 544 (1910).

20. Ibid., 367.

21. The court has defined a complicated test for fitting the punishment to the offense. The first requires evaluation of the gravity of the offence, which is supposed to be made "in light of harm caused or threatened to the victim or society" (as well as the culpability of the offender) (*Helm*, at 292). Though the Supreme Court has taken a greatly restrained view of its authority to enforce proportionality, and Congress and the state legislatures have retained responsibility for setting the range of punishments, by the time of *Weems* the principle of proportionality was already a part of American judicial thinking.

22. Pollock and Maitland have shown that classifying offenses for purposes of punishment was customary in English jurisprudence, and that lines of demarcation were guided by a measure of injury to the victim. They reported, "As to the thief's punishment, many old systems of law have at one time or another drawn two lines; they have distinguished between great and petty theft, and between manifest and non-manifest theft. He who is guilty of great and manifest theft is put to death in summary fashion; other thieves receive a much milder punishment." Exemplifying, they said that, "[i]n England both an old English and an old Frankish tradition may have conspired to draw the line between 'grand' and 'petty' larceny at twelve pence" (Sir Frederick Pollock and Frederic William Maitland, *The History of English Law before the Time of Edward I*, 2d ed. [Cambridge: Cambridge University Press, 1968], 495).

23. Blackstone's analysis of crime led to his suggesting such categories as "felonies injurious to the king's prerogative," "offenses aganist the persons of individuals," and "offences against private property." These different types of injuries were ranked according to severity in the rules that determined the specific punishments. Said Blackstone, "[T]reason in its consequences principally tends to the dissolution

drawing on these principles, the Revised Statutes of New York published in 1829,[24] had a classificatory system based entirely on the nature of the interest damaged and the extent of harm caused. In that New York Code, the few offenses that were defined as being the most serious were grouped together under the title "Of crimes punishable with death" (these were treason, murder, and arson in the first degree), and the few offences that were defined as being the least serious were grouped together under the title "Of offences punishable by imprisonment in a county jail, and by fines" (these included, for instance, "creating excess of steam in steamboats" and "physicians and others, when intoxicated, prescribing medicines").

The remainder of the offences were divided up by the nature of the interest damaged. After the title defining capital crimes came four additional titles—offences against the person, offences against property, offences affecting the administration of justice, and offences against the public peace and public morals—each of these punishable by imprisonment in a state prison. Within and between these categories, punishments were proportioned according to harm caused or threatened. Assault with a deadly weapon carried a penalty of imprisonment for a term of not more than ten years (Title 2, Sec. 36), whereas assault to commit a felony without use of a deadly weapon carried a maximum of five years (Title 2, Sect. 39). Grand larceny (theft of property valued at more than $25) carried a maximum of five years (Title 3, Sec. 66), whereas petit larceny (everything under $25) was limited to a term of six months (Title 6, Sec. 1). Proportionate fines were also provided for. Today, more than 150 years later, legislatures make virtually the same kind of grading systems for crimes, changing only the maximums and minimums set for the various categories.

This brief review should make it clear that the judges we interviewed, in giving such attention to the harm or damage caused by offenders, are expressing an interest very deeply rooted in Anglo-

---

of government, and the destruction thereby of the order of peace and society, thus denominates it a crime of the highest magnitude. . . . But there are crimes of an inferior nature, in which the public punishment is not so severe. . . . For instance in the case of battery, or beating of another" (Blackstone, *Commentaries*, book IV, sec. 5, p. 6, 2153–54).

24. The Revised Statutes of New York (1829), vol. 2, chap. 1, "Of Crimes and Their Punishment," title 7.

American legal culture.[25] The judges we studied are not historians, but they have lived in a legal system and have been trained in law schools that give voice to common cultural themes with respect to harm and punishment. As we will see in what follows, the judges express a set of fairly specific ideas about assessment of harm in white-collar cases.

The Assessment of Harm in White-Collar Cases and Common Crime Cases

It was not unusual for judges to speak about social harm or injury through statements comparing white-collar cases with two of the more frequent common crime cases that arise within the federal system, namely, drugs and bank robbery:

> There is a difference between peddling heroin which can destroy the lives of children, and the nonviolent, nondestructive . . . sort of activity which you see in white-collar crime. When you consider the impact the drug traffic has on society as compared to the impact that white-collar crime has on society there is just no comparison. A major drug dealer may be a source of supply for a thousand ultimate users, all of whom are hooked on drugs and all of whom are out committing crimes. . . . So one man can be responsible for untold muggings, burglaries, bank robberies, check forgeries, and so on. You don't have that in white-collar crime.

> The harm done by drugs, the harm and the inducement to general criminality, the effect of the drug market on any major city is tremendous. It induces crime. There are so many people who are committing armed robbery, burglaries, widespread criminal activity to sustain narcotics habits. That creates a tremendous danger, a tremendous cost to life in the city.

25. The question of what types of harm and how closely harm must be associated with punishment remains a central issue in the substantive criminal law. See, for instance, Stephen Schulhofer, "Harm and Punishment: A Critique of Emphasis on the Results of Conduct in the Criminal Law," 122 *U. Pa. L. Rev.* 1497 (1974), and Joel Feinberg, *The Moral Limits of the Criminal Law: Harm to Others* (New York: Oxford University Press, 1984).

Drug cases seem harmful because of the perceived effect of drugs in ruining lives and spurring other kinds of criminality. Drugs are seen as being a root cause of crime so that the drug dealer is responsible for the damage done to and by the user.

The other major category of ordinary crimes in federal courts is perceived as harmful because of the threat of violence. In the words of the judges,

> The person who embezzles ten grand is not likely to get the same penalty as somebody who walks into a bank with a submachine gun and robs it of ten grand. That type of offense doesn't warrant the same penalty. Going to a bank and holding a gun to somebody is more serious than embezzlement.

> _____

> There may be more money [in a price-fixing case] but you don't have these long-lasting traumatic effects on the individual that you do where a robber comes into a bank and puts a gun in a teller's face and the teller doesn't forget it for a number of years.

The Significance of the Absence of Violence in White-Collar Crime Cases

As these quotes suggest, one of the clearest badges of specific harm, danger, or injury is the presence of either the actuality or the threat of violence. Indeed, perhaps the single most common theme, when judges compared white-collar crimes with common crimes, related to violence:

> [White-collar defendants] are not people who are threatening the lives of others. They are not violent people.

> _____

> The most distinctive thing about white-collar crime is the lack of violence.

> _____

> Regardless of the amount, the element of violence overrides every other consideration.

> _____

> [White collar—non-white collar is not the important distinction] . . . a more proper distinction would be violent versus nonviolent and personal versus economic crime.

> _____

> A mugging with a knife or gun is certainly a much more antisocial

crime than the stealing of money from a bank where no one's life is threatened.

It is the street crime, the violent kind of crime which people are most concerned about. It is not the antitrust cases I get the letters about.

Only rarely did a judge's comment indicate any possible similarity between white-collar crimes and violent crimes. One judge in a southwestern state noted that the massive land fraud cases in which thousands of people lose their total life savings "are perpetrated by people who are just like the guys who hit you over the head." And more than one judge noted (as we shall see in the next chapter) that the highly deliberate and planned character of many white-collar crimes makes their perpetrators more culpable than defendants who may commit impulsive crimes with some element of violence. But the vast body of commentary and talk centers on the essentially nonviolent character of white-collar crime.

Thus a central element in assessing the seriousness of offense, namely, the presence of violence, is typically missing in the white-collar case. Violence, or its threat, makes an offense more serious because of the potential damage to persons that it poses. As one judge put it, "I think you have to deal with a violent individual differently than you do with one who is dealing only in economics because you are then talking about their interaction with another human being involving that other human being's life or liberty or well-being."

This state of affairs may change in the future, if the risks to life and limb inherent in the manufacture of defective automobiles or toxic wastes become more salient in judges' thinking about white-collar crime. At the present time, important as two or three highly visible cases may be, they do not seem important in the experience of our judges. Not one of them made mention of a case of that sort in our interviews.

The presence of violence and threats to persons clears the way for judges to impose severe punishment no matter what else is in play. One judge, in talking about the relative importance of violence and prior criminal record, put it this way:

> INTERVIEWER: So that lack of prior record cuts the same across white collar and non-white collar cases?

JUDGE: Not necessarily, I mean the first-time murderer I am not likely to put on probation. The first-time rapist I am not likely to put on probation. Any crime of violence, the first-time offender I am not likely to put on probation.

Another judge suggested,

Bank robbers. I've only in my whole life put two armed bank robbers on probation. All the rest are in prison. And usually for a long time. If you stop and talk about them, they are a kind of an interesting and important contrast with the white-collar person. The violent criminal is what I suppose the society is even more exercised about currently than the white collar. Scared, all of us. The judges included, I think, are scared. And the occasion for the relatively long prison term is most often present with that kind of criminal, where you have a feeling that one of the objectives you have to serve, one of the standard sentencing objectives, is incapacitation. As a dangerous person he will be locked up and he won't be waving and shooting guns at people for the period while he is locked up.

Still another judge described the importance of violence in the following way:

JUDGE: Violent criminals put people in fear, think they are going to be killed. They take hostages. They do all kinds of crazy things with a gun. All they have to do is snap that gun and boy, somebody is dead. Now what is worse to happen to anybody in this life, than death. You name it for me, or torture. It could be torture. And some of them do that even.

INTERVIEWER: You mentioned that also the robber—

JUDGE: They cut out tongues and balls and everything else. Violent crime, I am against. It is different than white-collar crime. . . . Even in black-collar crime if you want to call it that or bank robbery, but by God, I give them the works.

The absence of violence in white-collar cases has the additional consequence of requiring judges to distinguish between levels of harm without the benefit of the dimension of violence. This has the effect of elevating the significance of the other attributes of white-collar offenses for sentencing purposes.

Distinguishing among White-Collar Cases
on the Basis of Their Social Harm

The vast bulk of the judges' comments on the
seriousness of different white-collar offenses can be summarized under
one or another of four major categories: (a) the amount of monetary
loss, (b) the "spread" of the events over time and place, (c) the nature
of the victim, and (d) the presence and nature of violation of trust.

The Amount of Monetary Loss

Just as the amount of physical or psychological damage to the victim
can be used to assess the severity of a crime of violence, so the amount
of monetary loss can be used to assess an economic crime. Money
values are typically built into legislation, for example, in the distinction
between petty larceny and grand larceny. Thus it would be surprising
if the judges did not use monetary loss as a crucial element in assessing
the harm done by white-collar offenses. That they do consider monetary loss is shown in the following comments:

> Well, I think when you plead guilty to embezzling six hundred
> thousand dollars you don't have to go any further in determining
> what makes [the crime] serious.

> These guys had stolen a million dollars. You just can't ignore steal-
> ing a million dollars.

> What is the social harm? The social harm was the linking of double
> entry books by which he understated his income. But the amount
> was so small that I would have been able to demonstrate if I rep-
> resented him that the government wasn't deprived of a single dollar
> in taxes.

> [Explaining why a jail term was given in this particular case] You
> have a fraudulent scheme aggregating a million bucks. You just
> can't disregard that.

> If we are talking about a few hundred dollars or a couple thousand
> dollars the judge is not going to get as excited as he is going to get
> naturally if it is $100,000.

> The difference in the punishment [comparing a first offender ex-

ecutive who gets a longer sentence than a first offender check thief]
is not due to one being a white-collar crime and the other not. But
rather through one [the former] usually involving a great deal of
money where the latter does not. . . . There is symbolic value in large
amounts of money and you have to bring this symbolic measure to
the community by meting out a severe sentence.

If the amount of money is truly substantial, that fact may overwhelm
other features of the case that would suggest a less severe sanction.
A judge discussing a $750,000 swindle noted,

> In a major case, the severity of the crime can be such in a white-
> collar case as to overshadow the fact that this is a first offender with
> a nice clean background because of the major character of that
> offense.

In another case, a judge commented,

> If he hadn't paid income tax on a half a million dollars he would
> go to jail, whatever his previous station had been in the community.
> If it were a thousand dollars or so I wouldn't think that he would
> need much in the way of punishment. One who steals millions should
> be considered more seriously than one who steals thousands, at
> least as length of sentence is concerned.

Not one judge claimed that the amount of loss was either irrelevant
or of only minor significance, and most clearly give it a very heavy
weight. But how large a loss is a serious loss? If one were to generalize
from these interviews, there seems to be a consensus that amounts of
two thousand dollars and under are relatively small and would normally not require a severe sanction, while amounts in six figures or
more are serious and are likely to require incarceration. But there is
a lot of ground in between, and we suspect that some of the ambiguities
in white-collar sentencing, at least as they concern the amount of
economic loss, occur in the range upward of two thousand but short
of one hundred thousand dollars. Furthermore, as we shall see more
clearly in chapter 4, whether or not the defendant personally profits
from the loss and what he does with the profits also figure into the
calculus, although more in assessing the defendant's personal culpability than in assessing the seriousness of the offense.

Finally, there are ambiguities in assessing cost that are not resolved by simply knowing dollar values. Stolen securities, like stolen postal money orders, may be assessed at their face value or at their value on the street, which may be a tiny fraction of the face value. In a bribery case, is the economic loss to be assessed in terms of the price of the bribe and therefore the profit to the bribee or in terms of the value, typically much greater, of the benefit for which the bribe was paid? These and other ambiguities mean that even though there is agreement on the role of monetary losses or gains in assessing the significance of the offense, that agreement does not necessarily dictate a particular sanction. From the judges' point of view, this leaves room for appropriate individual discretion in sentencing, but from the perspective of the larger system such ambiguity may lead to arbitrary, inconsistent sentencing.

The Duration of the Offense

Many judges noted that white-collar crimes in particular are likely to be conducted over a long period of time and involve repeated violations. In addition to the total amount of loss such crimes create, the duration over which they take place is given an important place in assessing the harm done by the offense and hence the severity of the sanction:

> Normally most white-collar crime is a crime that's lasted over a period of time. The embezzlement has been going on for some time or the fraud, the scheme has been going on for some time. And they've been living off the fat of the land.

> [Discussing the case of a doctor inflating laboratory charges in connection with Medicaid programs]: His fraud went on over a period in excess of a year. The conduct was sufficiently flagrant and prolonged to justify a stiff sentence.

> It wasn't one transaction he was responsible for, it was for a number of notes, and banks and dealings . . . over a period of time and there was a long series of crimes involved.

> [Discussing a mail fraud case involving the solicitation of travel business]: This was a highly prolonged and fraudulent activity in which he had thrown all restraints to the wind.

[Discussing a tax case]: It depends... whether it is a pattern over several years or a one-shot deal. It is normally over several years because it takes that long to catch them and not having been caught he keeps doing it.

[Discussing a medicaid fraud]: I suspect because of the magnitude and the length of time — this went on for three or four years — I would have felt that a jail sentence was necessary.

The duration of offense is a much less obvious indicator of harm and seriousness than is the amount of monetary damage, and although it is clear from our interviews that duration is taken seriously, it is less clear precisely *why* it is taken seriously. In part it is because it suggests the repetitive nature of the crime in question; as in common crimes, repeaters are treated more severely than first offenders. On this score there is not a consensus among the judges. While many judges viewed long duration white-collar offenders as similar to the repeating common crime offender whose offenses are less patterned and take less time to commit, others took issue with that view. They argued that even though an offense may have been going on for years, it is the offender's first appearance in the criminal court that is the primary issue.

Duration was also seen as an indirect indicator of the degree of planning, calculation, and deliberateness that have gone into the offense and implicitly as a sign that the offense should be treated more seriously than offenses of the moment, in which rational calculation and planning play a lesser role:

[Discussing a case in which one company defrauded another company through a phony billing procedure]: I would have felt differently if they had put in one fake application... and that was all. To get up to a million dollars they probably had to put in as many as one hundred false applications. It does seem to me there is a greater moral responsibility for doing that thing and doing it again and again.

I tend to sentence more heavily in cases where the crime is continued over a long period of time, and appears not to be impulsive but rather willful and planned.

[Discussing a case of overbilling in which the victim was a foreign embassy]: There were a series of transactions, I believe a low of $245 and a high of $6,900 over the two-year period . . . so it indicated not an accidental overcharge, but a pattern of deliberate overbilling.

[Discussing an embezzlement case]: Another thing in aggravation was that the way this thing unfolded he was committing these acts over a period of two or three years or more so that he had guilty knowledge over all of this time, knew he was doing wrong, was committing crimes, was aware that he was committing crimes, as distinguished from an impulsive act of maybe stealing it in a twenty-four-hour period and trying to cover it up.

Duration obtains its importance from its use as a proxy for the repetitive and patterned nature of the offense on the one hand, the deliberate, calculating nature of the offender on the other. In this manner duration speaks directly to the ambiguity involved in trying to draw a precise line between the attributes of offense and the attributes of offender.

The Nature of the Victim

The judges gave much attention to the nature of victimization in white-collar cases. They are particularly concerned with whether, as one judge put it, "the victim actually incurs a loss." In most ordinary crimes both the victim and the loss are clear, but in white-collar cases often neither is clear. Indeed, several judges talked about white-collar crime as a type of "victimless" crime, and about the way that perception influenced their sentencing:

> INTERVIEWER: Is there anything particular about sentencing in white-collar cases which is difficult for you as opposed to other cases?
>
> JUDGE: Yes, I think there is, at least in this sense—there are certain sentencing procedures which don't trouble me nearly as much because it seems to me so apparent that a term in prison is essential from the point of view of the society. A crime accompanied by violence, either the threat or the actual harm to other people, or a crime which involves the trafficking of drugs, those people I almost invariably sentence to terms of imprisonment. The only question is how long the term should be. This can be a difficult question, but I find that somewhat less difficult

than the basic threshold question of does this man go to prison or is he admitted to probation. But I have very little trouble with recidivist armed bank robbers, or with someone who quite clearly is prepared to make as much money as he can out of trafficking in hard drugs. And generally speaking I think, I am less concerned and lose less sleep over that kind of situation than I do in the context of white-collar crime, because it is white-collar crime that—if I understand the term in the manner in which you mean it—you are dealing with nonviolent, non-injury-producing, so-called victimless crimes, and one doesn't find in that kind of crime some of the factors which incline me at least to think almost automatically of a term in prison.

[Discussing the case of an attorney found guilty of conspiracy to violate the immigration laws and making false statements—the attorney was arranging phony marriages between Chinese clients and U.S. citizens for the purpose of getting the Chinese clients admitted to the United States]: In non-white-collar crime cases, you have a clear sense of who has been hurt by the crime, whereas in white-collar cases it is not clear whether anybody has been hurt or what it means to talk about someone being hurt.

White-collar crime is more serious where there are visible and particular victims and where the relationship between offense and loss to the victim is direct. As one judge said,

Well, I suppose you had—you were a widow and a confidence man who had never been caught at anything before—I don't know whether he had committed anything or hadn't but he had never been caught. Gyp you out of your life savings and you are eighty-five years old and have no other thing, and this fellow had made a target out of you, knowing your weakness and how to get around to get the money out of your hands and so on. . . . Say about a fellow who does a reprehensible thing of that kind in a cold calculating way, whether it is his first offense or he is a recidivist, he is entitled to be reminded on a daily basis for a reasonable period what he has done.

This means that, in general, crimes like price-fixing and tax fraud are not likely to be regarded as seriously from the point of view of victimization because it is less easy to show particular, suffering victims. As one judge put it, one wants to distinguish pure economic crimes from those one-to-one relationships where "you put another person in jeopardy." This leads to a basic distinction, drawn by large numbers of judges, between the individual as victim and the organization or government as victim, with the latter category typically being viewed as less "victimized" than the former.

With respect to individual victims, there was a special concern for those that are viewed as being more defenseless, having fewer resources, or being in a weaker position to defend themselves. In the words of one judge,

> People who invest in investment companies come as close to being defenseless consumers as people can come. [The judge goes on to indicate how such consumers must depend upon the authenticity, honesty and accuracy of written documents describing new investment possibilities.] I had another defendant before me, a real bunko con man from an insurance company who was claiming to find loans for individuals in need of them. But he would require that they put down front money, fifteen, twenty thousand dollars front money. He promised that with this he would be able to secure loans of one hundred, two hundred, three hundred thousand dollars. There was simply a significant amount of fraud here. He will get more than eighteen months. . . . He moved around with people who had large sums of money. Look, in the last twenty years in this area [Los Angeles] the opportunities for establishing this type of life-style have grown tremendously in the Los Angeles area from becoming the type of person that lives off of exploiting others in a fraudulent manner. There are lots of people looking for legitimate money, but there are also a lot of people looking for illegitimate money around here now. You see the difference, this con man is deliberately ripping off widows, unsophisticated people, cripples. I am likely to look at this very differently than in other kinds of fraud.

Securities fraud is, in the opinion of many of the judges, the worst of the white-collar crimes because it hurts the innocent people who buy the securities. They have no way of protecting themselves.

Individual victimization is bad enough when it is based upon ignorance. It is even worse when the ignorant victim is also poor or dependent:

I sentenced a man the other day.... He had collected forty-three
million dollars and only accounted for forty-one million—two million missing. Several people had given him their life savings, para-
plegics, widows, orphans, and he had gone with them. He had sold
nonexistent interest in nonexistent condominiums allegedly located
in London. He went off with that money.... That is a white-collar
crime but a vicious sort of white-collar crime where poor people or
people who are dependent on money for their life savings turn it
over to some rascal like that who runs off with their money. That
is vicious.

[Discussing a securities case that involved selling interests in nonexistent cattle, on the justification for a prison term]: They were
taking money from poor people who had invested their life savings.

It is not simply that the victims are poor. In one case, a business
agent for a wealthy but incompetent and sick employer systematically
used his position to embezzle from the employer. The defendant received a prison term in part because he had stolen from a relatively
helpless victim.

But victims are not always in such a helpless position. One judge,
describing a case of mail fraud with SEC implications involving an
elder in the Mormon church, discussed the problem of identifying a
victim:

A lot of the time what happens to the prosecution of a white-collar
criminal is that sometimes the victim should be indicted also....
We studied the entire transaction and wondered why others were
not indicted and who was really the victim. One thing about the
traditional victim in a white-collar crime is that they also con the
conner. For that reason to categorize it as this defendant being a
white-collar criminal may not be too accurate. There are henchmen
in the group who are exploiting the so-called leader. Sometimes it
is very very difficult to make a distinction between who was the
wrongdoer or are they all wrong.... The indictment was returned
against the defendant white-collar criminal and also against some
of the henchmen but the other henchmen made deals with the government, both immunity from prosecution and so forth.... It is the
government, the prosecution that grants this immunity and I would
say out of four or five of the so-called white-collar criminal type

crimes that I have handled the government probably gave immunity to the wrong person, surely because they want to focus in on the person with the title so to speak, a church elder or whatever he is, the president of a certain company. The person may if you want to start talking in terms of degrees, be the least guilty.

One is reminded of the famous con man Yellow Kid Weil's remark: "I never stole from a person who didn't have larceny in his heart." But for every case in which the victim could be said to be implicated in the offense, there were many others where the individual victims are in the relatively helpless positions described above. This is what gives individual victimization its importance in locating the seriousness of offense.

By contrast, at least for most judges, neither large organizations nor governments can be perceived as being victimized in quite the same way. A core part of the general feeling of the judges is expressed in the following quotation:

> Where the government is defrauded the loss is spread over all the taxpayers in the country, whereas if you are defrauding—let's say a few investors or a particular employer, or embezzling money from a particular employer—then the loss is localized and I think that calls for a little more punishment then if you in effect spread the loss. There is a general feeling that it is alright to steal from the government because the government has got unlimited amounts of money and nobody is particularly hurt by it. And I guess there is a little of that same philosophy when it comes to sentencing.

Others echoed the sentiment in one or another form:

> The government is the one that suffers, not identifiable individuals who lose their life savings.

> [On the individual versus the institution as a victim]: The institution [in this case a bank] does not have a sense of individuality.

> [The taxpayer as a victim is] further removed from the offense than the victim buying stock.

> The difference is not giving what you owe to the government as opposed to taking something that doesn't belong to you from somebody else.

JUDGE [discussing a case of tax evasion]: He was up on four counts. That is $40,000. Well he could pay that out of his hip pocket. I knew it. But I said to the government, you are giving away the bank. But if that is what you want to do, OK, I will go along with you, because you don't have anything bad on this fellow. He hasn't cheated an individual, swindled orphans and so on.

INTERVIEWER: Whom had he cheated?

JUDGE: The government.

INTERVIEWER: So, it is important to you, how many victims?

JUDGE: Of course, it is important to me if the victim is an individual who is going to lose his whole life's savings. I am more concerned about that kind of a victim that I am about the government. The government is no victim. The government is just guilty of stupidity when they audited his tax account. They just had these young punks out of school who didn't know what they were doing, improperly audited.

Throughout our materials on victimization, then, there is a concentration on specific, individual victims to whom an identifiable harm can be shown to have occurred. Less weight is given to the nature of victimization when the victim is a massive organization, especially when it is the federal government itself.[26]

When one examines the range of offenses typically dealt with at the federal level, individual victimization is apparent in most forms of theft, for example, the theft of welfare checks from individual recipients, and in those securities frauds where individual investors are the victims. But in a large number of federal white-collar crimes—making false claims or statements to governmental agencies or to lending and credit institutions, engaging in bribery, or collusive price-fixing, or income tax fraud—victimization, at least of specific individual victims, is simply not evident. On occasion substantial sentences will be jus-

26. Some of the difficulties in the application of criminal law in the white-collar area stem from the heavily individualistic bias in our concepts of wrongdoing. We are here reporting the views of sitting judges, who have inherited the existing legal and cultural outlook. We have no specific alternative proposals, but it is at least worth asking whether a criminal jurisprudence begun anew in the age of organizations might not take a rather different shape and might not result in a rather different set of assumptions, and a different penalty structure, as regards offenses against individuals versus organizations. For a beginning, see the citations at note 14 of chapter 1.

MOUNT ST. MARY'S COLLEGE LIBRARY EMMITSBURG, MARYLAND

tified in cases where individual victimization is not evident, primarily on grounds of deterrence, but they will rarely be given on grounds of desert. It is much easier to perceive victimization when it takes very direct individual forms, and judges are probably not unlike the majority of citizens in thinking along these lines.

In one category, however, victimization can be seen as running far beyond the damage done to individual persons: crimes that are perceived as affecting or challenging the integrity of the larger social, political, or economic system. Almost invariably, those crimes are seen as involving a fundamental violation of trust.

The Violation of Trust

Positions in social life vary in the amount of responsibility they entail with respect to others. Where some special responsibility exists, the person may be regarded as holding a position of trust. For some judges the most distinctive feature of white-collar crimes is that they often involve persons in trusted positions, and this distinguishes them from common crime offenders. As one judge put it,

> White-collar cases pose special problems because they involve someone in a position of advantage—either a position of public trust or a high status position. To the extent that the white-collar criminal should be punished because he has betrayed a measure of social trust is valid, then the position he holds has something to do directly with the amount of trust he has betrayed.

Forms of possible trust violation are many and varied. Perhaps the clearest examples come from elected public officials holding public office:

> A public official who abuses his oath of office is a special criminal, who violates public trust.
>
> ———————
>
> In a political corruption case what you have is an abuse in which all of those who put the man in a position of power are really his victims. Political corruption cases are more like crimes of violence in which there are really clear victims than they are like other white-collar cases. Furthermore, like violent crimes, political corruption cases pose a real threat to the community. In income tax evasion cases or in government program fraud, people are simply stealing

public money. In political corruption cases they are endangering the very foundation of the government itself.

[Discussing a tendency to sentence persons in public office to prison]: It looks like inequality but I don't think it really is because people who put themselves in positions of public responsibility should probably have to bear a greater burden than others.

[Discussing the sentencing of a U.S. senator]: When you have a high government position, and you abuse it, steal from the government . . . I consider that much worse than if you are not employed by it and steal from it. In other words public trust, you violated your public trust.

But violations of trust are not limited to those who are in formally elected positions. Other government employees are assumed to accept a position of trust as a condition of their employment, and when they commit illegalities made possible by holding that position, they violate a public trust:

[Discussing a government employee who participated in a food stamp theft and resale to others, the total value of which was between ten and fifteen thousand dollars]: What was involved was abuse of position—taking an opportunity to steal that is similar to bank embezzlement.

In another case, an IRS official used the knowledge he gained in his position to engage in personal tax fraud, "a special kind of abuse of position."

If the government employee is also a law enforcement official, an additional burden of public trust may be entailed. In one case a prosecutor was involved in a marijuana smuggling ring: "I gave the guy ten years because I was really shocked that someone who was in the position of enforcing the law would get involved in such a heinous crime." And in the case of a fairly high-ranking woman on a police force who was convicted of welfare fraud and who received a three-year sentence, the judge said, "She had a special responsibility as a law enforcement officer."

Persons in the professions are another natural source for allegations of trust violation. In one case, a doctor dispensing drugs improperly was said by the judge to have abused his professional position. A

related argument concerns professional licensing. When another doctor engaged in medicaid fraud, a judge argued that physicians "are
licensed by the state of New York and that also added into the seriousness of it as far as I was concerned. . . . They are foisted on the
public."

And when the profession involves the distinctively moral qualities
of the priesthood or the church, an additional element of trust violation
is present. That was true in the case of the Mormon elder mentioned
earlier. It was also true for a minister who, using his position to run
a stolen car ring, had friends of the church selling hot cars:

> He was a man of the cloth—I think he was a minister rather than
> a priest—he was guilty of an inately evil performance in using his
> place to gain the confidence of others and then use that confidence
> in the scheme to line his own pockets substantially.

But abuse of trust is seen to run beyond these easily recognizable
categories, through many positions of major responsibility in organizations. It is viewed as intolerable when highly placed persons abuse
their positions. One judge explained his differing sentences to a number of persons involved in a scheme to loot their own company:

> Some of them were "important central officers." . . . I perceive a
> difference between someone who conducts and masterminds . . . to
> loot his own company of hundreds and hundreds of thousands of
> dollars, and someone he recruits to be a very minor soldier in this
> unworthy army . . . who doesn't have the position of trust in the
> company itself.

Another judge used military language to locate an exception to the
general rule that first offenders should be put on probation unless they
have committed violent crimes:

> JUDGE: This doesn't apply to the president of General Motors
> who [defrauds the government of] a million in income tax.
> INTERVIEWER: Why not?
> JUDGE: He's a colonel.

Another judge, describing his sentencing of a person who had been
"at the top of his banking profession" and for whom the judge rejected
a sentence of probation, said,

I think as an individual in a white-collar job moves up the ladder of success and is in a higher position of trust, the higher position of trust that he has obtained makes his crime more serious.

Finally, there are special obligations that befall those who work within an industry whose integrity is in theory guarded by special legislation, as in the case of the securities act:

It is serious in the sense that you have a whole industry, an investment company industry . . . that markets itself on making investments in securities available to the low- and middle-income person who cannot make their own investment decision. . . . They entrust their money. . . . The company is just a shell . . . it has a portfolio of securities. It has an outside investor who makes all the decisions. . . . The thrust of the Investment Company Act is that people who deal with that shell have a very high responsibility. This fellow who knew all about this violated this.

Taken together, these comments are indicative of the great importance attached to the concept of trust and trust violation in the sentencing of white-collar offenders. This heightened concern for trust and trust violation reflects more than the commonsense moral judgment that persons in responsible positions have a special obligation to behave responsibly. There is a sense that their violations damage the *fabric* of society in a way that others, even those who may employ violence as a means to their ends, do not. These injuries or harms represent a special form of victimization, unlike the victimization involved in taxpayer fraud or other efforts to cheat the government. One judge noted that in income tax evasion, people are simply stealing public money, whereas in political corruption "they are endangering the very foundation of government itself." Another, speaking of trust violation in a nongovernmental setting, noted that "the impact on society is more devastating I suppose. For that reason I think that punishment should be more severe." Another judge, commenting on the sentencing of a housing official at HUD who was accused of taking bribes from contractors, noted that the crime was "particularly serious." What made it so? The betrayal of public trust, for government officials are in a special category as white-collar offenders: "They have direct access to the power of the state, and when they abuse that power they threaten everyone in society." Thus, violation of a position of trust is seen to have an impact far beyond the immediate victims. The system itself is seen to suffer, thus increasing the harm done by the crime as well as the seriousness of the crime for society.

We began this chapter by noting that when they think about the sentence, judges are more concerned with assessing the harm done by an offense than with any other aspect of their cases. We argued that in focusing on harm, the judges participate in a long tradition that suggests the importance of harm in evaluating the severity of offenses, a tradition reflected both in the Anglo-American criminal law and in other cultures as well. Judges give primacy to harms done to specific and identifiable individuals and especially to harms that have a violent character. This distinguishes common crimes from most white-collar crimes, which lack the element of violence and often lack identifiable victims.

There is, nevertheless, a fairly broad consensus among the judges with regard to the assessment of the seriousness of offense. In giving content to the abstract category of seriousness or social harm in white-collar cases, the judges drew on commonsense moral judgments including many elements that are only implicit in the formal legal structure. Judges both expanded the concept of seriousness to include elements that are not necessarily spelled out in legislation and gave specific meaning to the differential seriousness of white-collar criminal acts by invoking the notions of monetary loss, of duration of offense, of victimization, and of trust violation.

Judges may vary in the weighting they give to each of these elements and in their detailed conceptions of how each should be defined and articulated. While these differences remain an important source of variability in sentencing from one judge to another, the more impressive finding to us is the extent to which, though using different words to express it, the judges hold a common view concerning the meaning and importance of harm in assessing the seriousness of offenses.

■ 4

Assessing the Offender: Blameworthiness and Criminal Responsibility

---

We begin with a rigid principle which charges him with all the evil that he has done, and then ... we accept first one. and then another mitigation of this rule.—Pollock and Maitland, History of English Law

In order for judges to arrive at what they feel is an appropriate sentence, they find it essential to locate defendants at least roughly in terms of their blameworthiness. They may or may not use the word *blameworthy* but, as we shall see below, they describe offenders and the differences between them in terms that enable an assessment of relative degrees of blame, fault, or responsibility. Not a single judge claimed to be able to sentence convicted offenders without regard to some such assessment. Indeed, characterizations of the offender along the dimension of relative blameworthiness, culpability, or responsibility would appear to loom at least as large in the judge's thinking as any of the other considerations in approaching sentencing. And although judges are likely to speak first of the harm or damage done by an offense, it appears that harm can be assessed in fewer dimensions or aspects than can blameworthiness.

As in the case of the harm or gravity of the offense, when the judges place blameworthiness at the center of their attention they are drawing upon a rich tradition in Anglo-American law. That tradition does not draw specifically on the word *blameworthiness*, but on a narrower conception of the states of mind necessary to find persons culpable or criminally responsible.[1]

---

1. Clearly the most central contemporary work on the relationship betwen mens rea and punishment is that of H. L. A. Hart. He states that a finding of a certain mental state is universally a condition of punishment in "civilized" societies. "All civilized penal systems," he writes, "make liability to punishment for at any rate serious crime dependent not merely on the fact that the person to be punished has done the outward act of a crime, but on his having done it in a certain state or frame of mind or will" (H. L. A. Hart, *Punishment and Responsibility* [New York: Oxford University Press, 1968], 114).

Criminal Responsibility
as a Core Legal Norm

When judges draw on concepts of moral blame-worthiness or responsibility to determine sentence, they reach back, as they do when they apply concepts of harm, into the early principles of the English common law and even further into ancient sources of law. A mishna of the *Babylonian Talmud*, for instance, makes the following distinction: "If one extinguishes the [sabbath] lamp because he is afraid of gentiles, robbers, or an evil spirit, or for the sake of an invalid, that he should sleep, he is not culpable. If because he would spare the lamp, the oil, or the wick, he is culpable."[2] Aristotle's *Nicomachean Ethics* expounds the central idea of moral culpability in conditioning responsibility on a requirement of voluntariness: "there will be things that are unjust, but not yet acts of injustice, if volun-tariness be not present as well."[3]

The idea of moral culpability is prominent in early English law also, though exactly how and when it was introduced is unclear. One inter-pretation suggests that the earliest law focused on the criminal act alone, not on moral culpability. In their history of English law, Pollock and Maitland wrote, "Law in its earliest days tries to make men answer for all the ills of an obvious kind that their deeds bring upon their fellows. . . . If once it be granted that a man's death was caused by the act of another, then that other is liable, no matter what may have been his intentions or his motives."[4] These authors argue that English criminal law evolved from a concept of absolute liability for criminal acts to include, around the start of the thirteenth century, a require-ment that certain defined mental states be found as a precondition to punishment.

Holmes disagreed with this interpretation of early English law. He found that there was always a clear concern in the laws of punishment for moral wrongdoing, not just for the causing of harm. He concluded,

2. *Babylonian Talmud*, Seder Mo'ed, Mishna, Shabbath 29b–30a, trans. I. Epstein (London: Soncino Press, 1938), 131.
3. W. D. Ross, trans. (Oxford: Clarendon Press, 1925), book V, chap. 8, as cited in Herbert Morris, *Freedom and Responsibility* (Stanford: Stanford University Press, 1961), 25.
4. Sir Frederick Pollock and Frederic William Maitland, *The History of English Law before the Time of Edward I*, 2d ed. (Cambridge: Cambridge University Press, 1968), 2:470–71.

"Our system of private liability for the consequences of a man's own acts, that is, for this trespass, started from the notion of actual intent and actual personal culpability."[5] The first system of criminal laws of a central government—called indictment and presentment—was based, said Holmes, on a similar view, that the perpetrator was guilty of moral wrongdoing. He found that the presentment was a "child of vengeance, even more clearly than the other [indictment]."[6] And vengeance implied personal moral culpability.

Others suggest that interest in the mental and moral status of the offender, though not explicit, was part of English law from its very origin. Professor Sayre asserts that throughout English history punishment was inflicted without *manifest* concern for examining intention or moral guilt, so that harm or conduct were made the primary conditions of punishment. Nevertheless, he argues that the concept of moral guilt was perceptible in the application of the early law, as if a harbinger of its full-blown presence shortly to appear. Thus he writes,

> But because the old records fail to set forth a mens rea as a general requisite of criminality one must not reach the conclusion that even in very early times the mental element was entirely disregarded. The very nature of the majority of the early offences rendered them impossible of commission without a criminal intent. . . . Furthermore, the intent of the defendant seems to have been a material factor, even from the very earliest times, in determining the extent of punishment. It was manifestly unjust that the man who accidentally killed with no intention of doing harm should suffer the extreme penalty of death.[7]

Whatever the early status of moral responsibility in England, important influences were felt in England by the end of the thirteenth century that were to have a fundamental impact on the developing criminal law, making concepts of moral blameworthiness absolutely central to the operation of the criminal law.[8] The first was that Roman law attracted new interest and was brought back into the curricula of universities in Europe, a movement that was relevant for the criminal

5. O. W. Holmes, Jr., *The Common Law* (Boston: Little, Brown, 1881), 4.
6. Ibid., 39–40.
7. Francis Bowes Sayre, "Mens Rea," 45 *Harvard Law Review* 974 (1931–32), 981.
8. Ibid., 982.

law because of the centrality of moral culpability in that tradition.[9] The second important influence was canon law, which made the notion of moral guilt into an overarching principle in the meting out of punishment.[10]

Sayre states that Bracton,[11] "whose book, written in the middle of the thirteenth century, powerfully influenced the shaping of the common law,"[12] relied heavily on canon and Roman law, and instead of just redacting the common law of his period, as appeared to be the object of his writing, brought in important principles from these sources.[13] One poignant example of this influence is the following passage from Bracton:

> We must consider with what mind (*animo*) or with what intent (*voluntate*) a thing is done, in fact or in judgement, in order that it may be determined accordingly what action should follow and what punishment. For take away the will and every act will be indifferent, because your state of mind gives meaning to your act, and a crime is not committed unless the intent to injure (*nocendi voluntas*) intervene, nor is a theft committed except with the intent to steal.[14]

The key place of moral blameworthiness becomes more prominent by the eighteenth century, and this can be seen in Blackstone. In describing the requisites of a crime, he included both will and act as essential elements, stating it this way: "[A]n *overt* act, or some open evidence of an intended crime, is necessary, in order to demonstrate the depravity of the will, before the man is liable to punishment. . . . So that to constitute a crime against human laws, there must be, first, a vicious will, and secondly, an unlawful act consequent upon such vicious will."[15]

The development of English law shows an expanding demand to find a "depraved" state of mind as a condition of criminal punishment. Before the modern period, the concept of intent thus implied a moral attitude, something like the mind's entry into sin. In the crime of

9. Ibid.
10. Ibid., 983.
11. Ibid., 984.
12. Ibid.
13. Ibid.
14. Bracton, *De Legibus* 101b, as quoted in Sayre "Mens Rea," 985.
15. William Blackstone, *Commentaries on the Laws of England*, book IV, sec. 20, p. 21, ed. William Carey Jones (San Francisco: Bancroft-Whitney, 1916), 2175.

homicide, this meant that a finding of murder required malice afore-thought, which then meant "an evil design in general; the dictate of a wicked, depraved and malignant heart."[16] And in larceny this meant that the taking had to be done *animo furandi*,[17] a term that also imported the idea of moral depravity. A natural accompaniment was the emergence of a set of exculpating justifications and excuses. If acts had to flow from a wicked mind to be criminal, then infants, persons forced to commit acts against their will, or persons so demented that they could not distinguish good from evil should not be found crim-inally responsible.[18] Sayre concludes that "by the second half of the seventeenth century, it was universally accepted law that an evil intent was as necessary for felony as the act itself."[19]

As the modern law of criminal responsibility has evolved, the lan-guage of vicious will or depraved state of mind has receded. More often, criminal intent is framed as a question of fact, the relevant issue being whether the defendant had knowledge of the likely consequences of the prohibited nature of his act.[20] If an act causes harm the person may be found culpable, according to one definition, where "it is his conscious object to cause the result," or "he is aware that it is prac-tically certain that his conduct will cause the result."[21] "Our modern objective tends more and more in the direction, not of awarding ad-equate punishment for moral wrongdoing, but for protecting social and public interests. To the extent that this objective prevails, the mental element requisite for criminality, if not altogether dispensed

16. Ibid., book IV, sec. 233, p. 198, 2403.
17. Ibid., book IV, sec. 271, p. 232, 2441.
18. Hart, *Punishment and Responsibility*, 13.
19. Sayre, "Mens Rea," 993.
20. In the modern law of substantive criminal liability there is a persistent am-biguity about criminal intent. In some jurisdictions, the normative aspect of criminal liability remains an integral part of the law. This appears to be true in California. In other jurisdictions, criminal intent is purely a factual and descriptive question. See George P. Fletcher, *Rethinking the Criminal Law* (Boston: Little, Brown, 1978): "The confusion between normative and descriptive language is so pervasive in Anglo-American criminal law that it affects the entire language of discourse. . . . When used normatively, 'criminal' refers to the type of person who by virtue of his deeds deserves to be branded and punished as a criminal. When used de-scriptively, as in the phrase 'criminal act,' it may refer simply to any act that the legislature has declared to be 'criminal' " (397).
21. Sec. 2.02(2)(a)(i) and sec. 2.02(2)(b)(ii), *Model Penal Code*, Official Draft and Explanatory Notes as adopted at the 1962 Annual Meeting of the American Law Institute (Philadelphia: American Law Institute, 1985).

with, is coming to mean not so much a mind bent on evil-doing as an intent to do that which unduly endangers social or public interest."[22]

Despite this general shift in the technical meaning of criminal responsibility, our law continues to return to the morally laden language of criminal intent. Thus Bishop, a leading American commentator on criminal law, has used the emotionally charged language that dominated in an earlier period, thereby showing that it is probably more correct to think of both the older and the modern doctrines as strands of a common thread. That thread contains elements of moral concern as well as the analytic view that focuses on the foreseeability of consequences. Wrote Bishop in his leading test, "The doctrine which requires an evil intent lies at the foundation of public justice. There is only one criterion by which the guilt of men is to be tested. It is whether the mind of men is criminal."[23]

A modern reference to the older concept of intent can be seen in the leading decision of the Supreme Court in *Morissette v. U.S.*, decided in 1952.[24] There Justice Jackson found that a man charged with stealing under a new federal statute was entitled to have the jury decide whether he had knowledge that the taking of abandoned government property from open government land was illegal. Though mens rea was for this court strictly related to knowledge of circumstances, Justice Jackson emphasized that the Court was remaining true to the historic idea of crime as springing from an "evil-meaning mind."[25] Rejecting the argument that there could be absolute liability in a statute prohibiting taking of government property, Justice Jackson said,

> The contention that injury can amount to a crime only when inflicted by intention is no provincial or transient notion. It is as universal and persistent in mature systems of law as belief in freedom of the human will and a consequent ability and duty of the normal individual to choose between good and evil. . . . Unqualified acceptance of this doctrine by English law in the Eighteenth Century was in-

22. Sayre, "Mens Rea," 1017.
23. Joel Prentiss Bishop, *Commentaries on the Criminal Law* (Boston: Little, Brown, 1882), p. 171, sec. 287.
24. Morisette v. United States, 342 U.S. 246, 72 S. Ct. 240, 96 L.Ed. 288 (1952).
25. Ibid., 251.

dicated by Blackstone's sweeping statement that to constitute any crime there must be a "vicious will."[26]

As our interviews show, the moral character of the person who committed the crime has remained an important part of our system of criminal sanctions. Though it has largely been excluded from the guilt determining stage of the criminal process—except to the extent that knowledge of circumstances and foreseeability of consequence is taken as a surrogate or mechanistic formula for expressing a moral definition of wrongdoing—it is very much a part of the sentencing stage. Judges go beyond the limited moral texture of the contemporary substantive criminal law, expanding their inquiry so that they evaluate many features of a case that touch on a broad measure of moral blameworthiness. In doing so, judges seem to be using moral blameworthiness not only as a measure of deservedness of the sentence for the particular individual charged, but also as an indication of injury caused to society. Judges seem to say something like this: The more greedy and calculating is the crime, the more it undermines the social fabric; it thus requires the use of greater deterrent force for the protection of society. In so saying, our interviews suggest that judges reach back to the classical concepts of the criminal law, and in doing so bring a degree of order and reliability to a decision otherwise unbounded by rules.

The Expansion of Responsibility into Blameworthiness

As most of the judges see it, the legal conditions for establishing guilt and criminal responsibility are an important starting point, but only a starting point for assessments of blameworthiness. The judges say, in effect, We know the offender was legally responsible, but was he *really* responsible? We know that he had the requisite intent to commit a crime, but how intentional was it really? We know the offender was culpable but in deciding on a sentence we have to ask, *How* culpable?

In beginning to answer these questions, the judges expand the concept of criminal responsibility into one that comes closer to moral

26. Ibid., 250.

blameworthiness. This expansion allows them to consider attributes of blameworthiness that go far beyond those relevant to establishing guilt in a criminal trial, although assessment may begin there. They are likely to start with events surrounding the offense itself, to provide some preliminary indicators of the defendant's blameworthiness. They then move both backward and forward—backward chronologically to an assessment of the defendant's past conduct, his personality, his motivational structure, and many attributes of his personal and social history. The assessment may then move forward chronologically to include character readings based upon the defendant's conduct after the offense but preceding sentence, to include such elements as the presence or absence of cover-up, of lying or deceitfulness, of remorse, of cooperation with the prosecution and the like.

Now of course not all of these attributes will be relevant in every case, nor will they all be relevant for every judge. And although virtually any element of past conduct or present behavior might conceivably be used as an indicator of blameworthiness, there appear to be a recurring series of categories that are used by many judges, suggesting a patterning and consistency in thought that may not be evident when the focus is on individual differences among judges. We shall examine each of these elements in detail below, after considering one quality that looms large in the judges' minds when they distinguish white-collar from common crime offenders.

The Special Status of the Defendant's Prior Criminal Record

It is well established in criminal law that the prior record of an offender is a crucial, some would say *the* crucial, attribute of the defendant's background that should be considered at the time of sentencing. Some legislative enactments provide longer penalties for repeaters than for first offenders, and there are "habitual criminal" statutes that require defendants, even those convicted of minor crimes, to be sentenced to long terms of imprisonment. Thus it is hardly surprising to find that judges give a great deal of attention to the prior record of the defendant when they decide upon a sanction. A large number of our judges noted that the most distinctive difference between white-collar and common crime offenders was the absence of a prior record among most white-collar defendants:

The one thing that is true of the so-called white-collar criminal is that invariably you have a defendant who is being sentenced for the first time and that is always difficult. It is always difficult to find the appropriate sentence in a criminal case involving a person who has never had a contact with the criminal law before. [This judge felt that prior record was the only feature that in general distinguished white-collar from common crime offenders.]

The white-collar defendant "usually is an individual who has never before been convicted or never before been accused."

But what is it about the prior record that makes it so significant? For some judges it is simply obvious that the first offender deserves a break at sentencing:

If it is their first offense normally . . . the first offense I put them all on probation—second offense, I probably send them to jail.

———

[Discussing sentencing of first-time tax violator—not too serious but a violation nonetheless]: Well, generally if it was certainly his first offense you would put him on probation. I would. Why not?

Others see prior record as a basis for making an assessment of moral character:

The prior record says to me . . . particularly if he has gotten a light sentence or probation before, he has been given a chance and hasn't profited by it. Indeed [it] probably led him to believe that he could commit another crime without punishment, and when you are deal-ing with that sort of mentality you are virtually required to say the second time, you had your one chance and now you are going to pay for it.

———

[Discussing prior record in a robbery case]: It causes me to believe when I come to sentence him, hey look fellow, you have already taken a bite of the apple, now you have swallowed the core. You should be punished because I know you knew better. That is what prior record means.

———

[Discussing a woman convicted of welfare fraud who in the past had been arrested and convicted six times, and each time put on pro-bation. Even though the amount of the offense was $24.68 he sent her to jail]: The slap on the wrist hadn't worked—this woman needed a jar.

If a person has a prior record, you have a right to assume that his protestations are not sincere—if he has had one chance to straighten himself out.

The first time you get caught and you face the clanging doors, you are probably to be considered for more lenient treatment than if you have once been apprehended and sentenced and now you have sinned again.

The presence of a prior record signals to judges that they are dealing with a kind of person who may be incorrigible or a habitual criminal. In either case it is clear that such persons are thought to merit more severe treatment.

For other judges, the first offense was important less because of what they could infer about the offender's sincerity or capacity to learn, but more because the first offense is likely to be situationally induced, and the defendant an unlikely repeater.

Typically you are dealing with a first offender, and it is not quite the same as the third or fourth conviction of someone who either knocks over banks or peddles drugs for a living, and is quite clearly going to go on doing so if you give him the opportunity.

[Comparing two drug dealers, otherwise equal in culpability, one with six convictions, the other with none.] The first was given "a generous benefit of the doubt" at the time of sentencing. The judge felt it important to protect people from criminal activity, and the person with six convictions is more likely to repeat than the one without any prior record.

[Discussing a bank vice-president who has a business on the side that is in trouble financially and who juggles the books to salvage the failing business. It just happens that at that time there is an audit and he is caught]: A guy like this will never get in trouble again, obviously.

Although virtually all judges attach some significance to prior record, there are a number of qualifiers. Some went to the irrelevance of the prior record if it was unrelated to the present offense:

[The prior record may be a predictor of future conduct]: But that assumption only works where the prior record is for the same type of crime as that for which the defendant would be presently convicted.

Another set of qualifiers concerned factors that may conflict with prior record, such as the seriousness of the offense, the amount of money involved, or the duration of the offense:

There is almost a presumption of probation in a white-collar offense the first time around unless it is a very egregious offense. Or a great deal of deliberateness and a great deal of money is involved.

[Discussing a person convicted for the first time after seven years of committing white-collar illegalities]: The fact that he doesn't have a prior record isn't important because the act which he committed shows the same kind of knowledge and deliberation as a prior record supports in [a robbery case].

Still others wonder whether the "official" prior record is an indication of the defendant's true prior history, though they do not necessarily act on this doubt in the same way:

Most of the white-collar crime that comes to me it is for the first time.... I'm sure that the probabilities are that he has been doing something illegal or stealing money and just hasn't gotten caught. But that is a supposition that I can't make, and add to the sentence.

[A judge notes that in non-white-collar cases he pays minimal attention to the prior arrest record unless it is followed by a conviction, whereas in white-collar crime cases]: If there are some facts that indicate that maybe somebody did something but wasn't convicted, I will take the facts into consideration.

The absence of prior record in most white-collar cases places the sentencing judge in a difficult position. If he should treat its absence as he would in most common crimes then white-collar criminals will be treated in a uniformly more lenient fashion. As one judge said,

In other crimes there is a general feeling that a first offender shouldn't be sent to jail. In white-collar crimes that would in essence give a defendant a license to commit crime because typically white-collar criminals are first offenders . . . and so I have a general feeling that white-collar criminals should get some jail time.

Should the absence of a prior record be disregarded, then greater severity would result. Indeed some judges believe that that is already the case.

Of course, whether in fact white-collar defendants are more likely to get jail time is an empirical question that we do not address within the body of this study.[27] But the general significance attributed to prior record as an element in sentencing cannot be doubted. And quite apart from what judges actually do or feel they should do, they clearly find it easier to send a person to prison if the person has committed a violent crime, or if the person has a long record of prior convictions. Sentencing a nonviolent first offender to prison is a wrenching experience. One judge stated what was implicit in a number of commentaries: "I feel more of an emotional tug [when sentencing a first offender to prison]. You *see* the impact on him. He has never thought of going to jail in his life." It would appear to be this emotional constraint that at least gives judges pause before sentencing a first-time white-collar defendant to incarceration, even if they believe that an incarcerative sentence may be justified on other grounds.

The main point of this extended discussion of the role of the defendant's prior record is to show that, like violence in the case of assessing the seriousness of offense, judges must assess the blameworthiness of white-collar defendants without appealing to that most familiar basis for differentiating offenders, namely, prior record. The absence of prior record enhances the importance of the other qualities of offenders that may lead some to be seen as more and others as less blameworthy. In our discussion, we deal first with elements or indicators of blameworthiness that emerge from the crime itself of from its immediate context, then with those elements that characterize the prior history of the defendant, and finally with those that become evident to the judge during the process of indictment, trial, conviction, and sentencing.

27. Stanton Wheeler, David Weisburd, and Nancy Bode, "Sentencing the White Collar Offender: Rhetoric and Reality," *American Sociological Review* 47 (Oct. 1982):641–59.

Assessing Blameworthiness: Evidence from the Offense and Its Immediate Context

Knowledge and Intent

One important way in which legal categories get expanded into the judges' moral assessment of the offender is through a simple extension of the legal culpability requirements. Was this person really aware that he or she was committing a crime? Was there real intent on the person's part? Answers to such questions are difficult enough to establish in cases where there is a smoking gun, missing jewels, and the like. In white-collar crimes, they may be especially difficult. Defense lawyers seek to exploit the ambiguity of many white-collar offenses to try to create doubt in the minds of judges about whether even the narrow requirements of legal responsibility have, in fact, really been established.[28] In many cases this strategy clearly meets with a sympathetic response. Thus one judge, explaining what information he needs to have in a tax fraud case, commented as follows:

> I want to be really sure that this was fraud. There are situations, I've seen them defending tax cases and prosecuting them, where a guy definitely didn't pay all the taxes he owed, but where there is considerable doubt, was it really willful fraud or was it just sloppy bookkeeping; maybe in some vague sense that maybe I'm not paying everything I owe, but I'm probably pretty close, and then it turns out you were $30,000 off. Is it that kind of a case, or is there just no doubt that this guy knew?

Another case involved a banking regulation violation in a small town, where the bank lost some fifty thousand dollars. In the judge's words,

> There were four people indicted. I didn't feel that any of them were criminals. I didn't feel that any of them had—were intentionally

28. Kenneth Mann, *Defending White-Collar Crime* (New Haven and London: Yale University Press, 1985). This same set of concerns elevated beyond the individual case raises the question of the advisability of using the criminal sanction in some of these areas. Alternative remedies exist in the arsenel of sanctions possessed by the federal government: administrative remedies, tort recoveries, and so on. The criminal sanction implies nothing if not moral condemnation, and if culpability is frequently doubtful in these cases, perhaps other sanctions would be more appropriate.

culpable. But I felt that their informality in following the banking regulations reached a point where it was flagrant informality, but nobody set out to—nobody lined his own pocket, for example. . . . These fellows never had criminal intent—they just loaned money without requisite collateral, or financial statement. . . . And they just got so damned informal on this that eventually some people in the town started taking advantage of it, and all of a sudden they came up with loans they had to write off, and there was absolutely no justification for having made them on the terms on which they made them.

A judge discussing a veterinarian who cheated on his income tax explained a three-year sentence in terms of

the quality of guilt, so to speak. . . . [He asks,] What *scientor* did he have at the very outset, from the beginning, all through the period that this occurred what *scientor* did he have that continued through the trial of the case? [The judge could sense from his testimony that he was intentionally falsifying books.]

On the Degree of "Deliberateness" or "Scheming"

Even when the defendant's actions have passed the legal test of willfulness necessary to establish legal guilt, this provides only the beginning of the judge's attempt to assess the degree of culpability of the defendant. Their language frequently speaks of the degree of scheming, planning, deliberate and calculated activity as an indicator of the blameworthiness of the defendant. Thus:

If he was involved inadvertently—I think I would take that into account. . . . [But] what was involved was a *master scheme*.

A big part of what happened related to exactly who did what in connection with falsifying the statements. There were certain activities that involved the literal production of some accounting records so that accountants could see them. Writing out false accounting records. And who was responsible for doing that, for directing that it be done? . . . There is a difference between somebody sitting in a dark room and manufacturing accounting records, and another case where it is sort of an exaggeration or misleading language. You know, there is a difference in culpability.

The judges clearly assessed the offenders' conduct using standards broader than those that would be acceptable in the courtroom itself. Indeed, sometimes the defendant's conscious effort to walk the thin line separating legal and illegal activity is taken as a sign of the defendant's blameworthiness. How all of this may result in a judgment of deviousness, a judgment of character, is indicated in the following exchange:

INTERVIEWER: Could you point out what specific thing that you learned in the trial led you to feel that it was a more serious crime or that you should give more—a longer sentence than you might have given otherwise.

JUDGE: Well, I thought I indicated that.

INTERVIEWER: The defendant—I guess I don't understand what he did.

JUDGE: Well, he was head of the company, he was chairman of the board of a discount store, and they issued quarterly financial statements and on one or two of the quarters, maybe three of these quarterly financial statements, he procured his underlings to falsify the records and falsify the financial statements. Do you understand?

INTERVIEWER: Yes.

JUDGE: Okay, and after—so he got, he didn't do it himself, he didn't do the dirty work himself, he got other people. And he did it by not literally standing there and saying, "You go and falsify the financial statements," he said things that would hopefully signal to them to do the thing, but if he was ever quoted it wouldn't sound— a jury might say, well he didn't do this. In other words if I say to you, I under the right circumstances—if you are the controller of a company, and I say to you, "Look you go and you make up a lot of phoney accounts receivable entries" so that you will, and then you use that to inflate the assets on the upcoming quarterly financial statement and inflate the earnings. If he ever comes into a trial and quotes you, then that is very damning. Now under the right circumstances I could say to you, "I want our earnings increased by $800,000." Under the right circumstances that is a signal to you to falsify something, but if it is ever quoted against me I can come back and say I didn't mean to have any falsification by anybody, I was just telling him that I wanted us to work harder to earn all this money. So I have used a kind of code to insulate myself if I can against criminal liability. That is a very devious thing.

Another judge suggested that in making such assessments he had to look beyond the formal record to see what really went on:

Very frequently you end up with an indictment with a large number of counts and every one of the counts is nothing more or less than the mailing of a letter. It doesn't give you a real appreciation of the magnitude of the scheme . . . whether he was drawn into the scheme or plotted it out, whether after he realized he was involved in a full-scale fraudulent scheme he tried to get out of it or continued full steam to milk it . . .

In a tax fraud case involving double bookkeeping, a father and son are distinguished for sentencing on grounds of the greater deliberateness and culpability of the father:

JUDGE: Well there is no question about it, but his was a scheme, a well worked out scheme. It wasn't one that just accidentally happened, or wasn't carelessness, or it wasn't just inconvenience.

INTERVIEWER [later]: There was no vagueness in the case at all?

JUDGE: No vagueness whatsoever. He deliberately set up and worked out a scheme, and had been conducting it for years. And his son came in and he said, "Son, this is the way we work it. We don't pay more taxes than we want to, and we work it this way." And he taught his son to do it.

Even if the amount of money involved in an offense is substantial, a reading of the deliberateness of the defendant still seems relevant:

INTERVIEWER: I guess I have a little difficulty with that concept because I am wondering, if the damage is a million dollars, what is the difference if it is a scheme of this type or that type?

JUDGE: The difference is in the degree to which a person should be punished and deterred. You can blunder accidentally into a loss, occasion a loss to somebody else, but when you start out to do it deliberately and you get to the same result—the impact merely spells the fact that there has been a violation somewhere along the line.

But sentencing has to do with selectivity—picking out the appropriate sentence for the degree of culpability.

It is the fit between the degree of culpability and the severity of punishment that is crucial. Judges engage in a mental operation parallel to the operation involved in the assessment of harm.

One further statement characterizes a theme that occurred in other interviews:

What I am driving at is that the degree of culpability, and that is what you attempt to ascertain in the sentencing process, may importantly depend on the deviousness and the schemes employed to indicate the unlawful intent involved. To the degree that there is that procession of devious conduct and cessation of devious conduct you begin to measure the degree of culpability of the individual for ultimate sentencing. I had another case here not so long ago—some years back—where there was a flooding of an area in Pennsylvania (I think it was) and claims were made to the government and the state for disaster losses. And what these fellows did was to go out and bomb particular little areas and make the thing look like a disaster and collect the money. So that you see it wasn't merely the fact that they had filed false claims but the manner in which they did it indicated the level of their misconduct, and that weighed into the quotient of what the sentence should be. I had forgotten what the congressional limit of time was on the thing, but you get closer when you start in from zero say to ten years you get closer to ten years if you find somebody has thought the thing through on all its angles and worked out a scheme of conduct as contrasted with somebody who just happens to flop into the enterprise and make a false statement. The false statement itself may be the crime to be punished, but the deviousness with which they may have arrived at that false statement may have important impact on the quantum of confinement to be fixed.

Again we are taken back to deviousness and to the way scheming and planning is read as creating a greater degree of blameworthiness.

Relative Culpability among Multiple Defendants

Perhaps the clearest readings of culpability or blameworthiness are found in those instances, frequent in the white-collar crime

area, in which multiple defendants have been involved in an offense. In these cases one often finds that judges will have spent a
good deal of time sorting out the role that each defendant played,
their relative contribution to the offense, and will use this relative
ranking as an important basis for discriminating between one and
another defendant with respect to the sentence. Consider the following cases:

> [Describing a complex forgery and fraud in which counterfeit cash-
> ier's checks are used to buy large items. The scheme involved the
> person who conceived the idea and organized the fraud, the printer
> who made up phoney cashier's checks, and the various persons used
> to actually carry out the transactions. The judge is describing why
> the first of these got a longer sentence]: Well I thought his problem
> was more severe because he—one, he was involving a lot of people.
> He tried to keep himself out of it. What he did was send people
> out to do these things—here is a woman who looks as if she had
> money and so when she would go out to these people, with a chauf-
> feur-driven car, to look at a Cadillac, of course they think she really
> has money, and that is how he would get the Cadillac. Also he was
> dealing with gold coins. He masterminded it and I thought that
> therefore he ought to take the greater brunt of it. One man only
> had been involved in it peripherally, and I think I gave him about
> one year, or two years. The printer I thought was more culpable
> next to the mastermind, more culpable because the scheme couldn't
> be carried out without him. So I think that is why I gave him five
> years. [The organizer got a little more.]

> I think it all turned [the variations in sentences for persons convicted
> of the same offense] in that case on the relative culpability of the
> defendants.... I think degree of culpability is of course always
> about the number one thing to look at.

> There were two brothers, they ran the business. One brother got a
> lesser sentence than the other, but one brother was more involved
> with machinations than the other. There was a lawyer—he got as
> long a sentence as the first brother, the longer-sentenced brother.
> He got a year, because he and that brother were ring leaders in this
> thing.... An accountant, who sort of got drawn into this... was an
> underling and he certainly didn't originate any of it.... The problem

of the subordinate whose job is at stake and who is dragged in more or less willingly is different from that of others.

Where I have had multiple defendants I think I really kind of lay them out in terms of severity of sentence which may not always turn always [*sic*] on culpability. . . . There are other distinguishing things, such as previous offenses. . . . I tend to lay them out on that table or someplace. . . . Maybe I go from highest to lowest, maybe I don't. . . . I go back and forth and I lower this and raise that, but I think that in that particular case, I'd probably decided that ____ought to get a year and ____ought to get a year, and we sort of went down from there.

I had a case . . . within the last year or so against an investment banker. . . . The charge was that he had gained control of a discount house business, and that the discount house business was failing, it was turning out pretty badly. And he—the charge was that he persuaded, directed, instigated the falsification of financial statements. This was a public company. And the financial statements would of course be used by potential lenders, investors, and so forth. He was convicted, up for sentencing. . . .

Now a big part of what happened related to exactly who did what in connection with falsifying the statements. There were certain activities that involved the literal production of some accounting records so that accountants could see them. Writing out false accounting records. And who was responsible for doing that, for directing that it be done. How long did this go on? At what time did certain people begin to have some qualms and one of them ultimately told the accountants about the problem? It was a very complex story. And [at the trial] you got a very—in the first place you knew where the complexities were and where the things were that were clear, that all in all you knew a lot of evidence relating to precisely what the deeds were, how culpable they were. There is a difference between somebody sitting in a dark room and manufacturing accounting records, and another case where it is sort of an exaggeration or misleading language. You know there is a difference in culpability.

[Describing the sentencing in a complex counterfeit stock fraud operation]: As far as those who pleaded guilty and either testified or did not on the trial, one I put on probation. He had participated, but he was a younger man, quite unsophisticated, a manipulee rather than manipulator with no prior criminal record, so I put him on probation for two years and told him to get out of New York City and go back to Wyoming where he had come from. There was [*sic*] older men who, one of whom had had some prior difficulties with the law. Others had not but were executive-type people, manipulators at the very heart of the scheme, and they received prison terms.

The same judge elaborated on a longer sentence in another case:

His role was great—his machinery, facilities, were essential; his account used for deposit and distribution; his offices were used; . . . also he participated quite handsomely in the proceeds of the scheme and my feeling was that he was a very important participant and that also he was in a position to appreciate the very real degree to which this kind of market business depends on trust, on the genuineness of documents, on the trust you can have in peoples' words.

And still later:

I perceive a difference between someone who concocts and masterminds, implements a scheme to loot his own company of hundreds and hundreds of thousands of dollars, and someone who he recruits to be a very minor soldier in this unworthy army off in Miami who doesn't get nearly as much money out of it and doesn't have the position of trust in the company itself. Now that is not to say that you have a license to steal or assist in the theft from a company in which you are not an officer or of which you are not an employee—the man committed a crime and was convicted for it. But I do think that in the sentencing process you can take into account these differentials.

In complex frauds that require both a special, trusted position and participation in the fraud, these central elements may not necessarily work together. But here is a judge explaining what happens when they do:

Speaking generally there are separate factors I suppose. One, participation in the conspiracy itself, the criminal act, and two, the position within the hierarchy of the institution that winds up being the victim. The maximum combination of factors pointing toward incarceration is where, as in this case, the two come together. The individual in question is both a senior, trusted officer and one of the architects of the criminal scheme. And when those factors come together in one individual, I should think, a sentencing judge would be more inclined to incarceration on a relatively longer rather than a shorter term than otherwise.

But the presence of multiple defendants does not always lead to differentials in sentencing. Sometimes the role of the defendants is so similar there is no basis for distinguishing them. In discussing defendants who had made false statements in connection with a loan application, a judge commented,

> In this case, there was no question that there was equal responsibility. There was absolutely no basis for distinction. The social situation of the two defendants were almost exactly the same. They were both married. They both had children. The whole bit. It was the same, so I never had any doubt in my own mind in that case once I became acquainted with the facts that there was no reason not to impose the same sentence in each situation. But I have stock fraud cases, for example, for which I have imposed quite different sentences on the defendants in the same case.

Those judges who commented on the assessment of relative culpability in non-white-collar cases argued that the process was much the same—there are different degrees of participation in a bank robbery and in a drug transaction just as there are in complex white-collar cases. But at least one judge thinks that it is often more difficult to assess the exact role of the defendant or their level of responsibility in white-collar as compared with common crime cases. He said,

> If you put it into a price-fixing context, it's extremely difficult because the whole corporate process like the governmental process with its committees and its memoranda and its recommendations and debates diffuses responsibility to the point where ultimately it's almost impossible to fix, but if it is two or three people who clearly got together and did something . . . You do that in sentencing all the time. You are always establishing the relative degrees of guilt in giving different sentences to people involved in the same crime.

It's very common in narcotics cases to the extent that they even have a nickname for the guy. You get a delivery of heroin, a big delivery of heroin, the guy walks in the room and lays down a bundle and picks up $50,000. Sounds like a big crime, but this guy is the mule, he gets $200 to deliver, and they even call him the mule, and the guy who is really involved is the buyer. It's the buyer on the one hand, the guy who sold it on the other hand, and the guy who cut it and all the people really involved in the deal and the mule is just some mope they picked up in some bar and said if you deliver this package we will give you $200. You are always trying to assess the levels of responsibility when several people are involved in the crime. As I said, in the corporate structure, it becomes almost impossible because it diffuses so, but in the simpler crimes, it's usually fairly easy.

Assessing Blameworthiness: Evidence from the Life History of the Offender

Important as the defendant's conduct during the commission of the crime may be, it provides only one basis or anchoring point for an assessment of the appropriate sentence. The judges share a basic agreement with the philosophy of individualized sentencing that makes a whole host of past personal attributes of potential relevance to the sentencing decision. One judge put the general argument as follows: "In weighing what you want to do with a particular individual defendant, I don't think you can focus solely on the particular crime which he stands before you on. You have got to view his whole life history and his place in society."

While virtually all of our judges would ascribe to this view in some degree, there is no single list of attributes or qualities that are believed decisive, and no single attribute gets considered in isolation from the others. Rather, there is a complex mixture of character-revealing traits, some stemming from life history, others from judgments with regard to more stable personality characteristics, still others from assessments of motive.

Some suggestion of the complexities involved in weighing these various features is revealed in the following two quotes that speak to the relevance of military record:

I have had ... cases where the defendant was a wounded, decorated veteran of war. ... If somebody makes sacrifices for his country that is on the plus side and you have to weight it with the negative things he has done and you don't just focus on the crime, you have got to look at everything in his life.

JUDGE [discussing the sentencing of a major political figure convicted of bribery]: He was convicted by the jury, and in view of his status, education and what not, I gave him the maximum sentence.

INTERVIEWER: Why?

JUDGE: I had an army background. I always felt a colonel should receive a heavier penalty for the offense than a private. [He had] all the advantages in the world: a wealthy family, society, a fine education, fine background. Of course he did have a wonderful war record which I didn't let weigh too heavily in his favor or I would have turned him loose the first time, but the other things I felt overweighed it.

There appears to be a widely shared set of judgments about the general qualities that should "count" in an assessment of character, although there may not be agreement on the precise weight each should receive. In our analysis of the judges' comments, we first divide them broadly into three major categories: statements pertaining to life history or circumstances, statements pertaining to personality, and statements pertaining to motive. These are in roughly ascending order chronologically as we move from background up to the situations preceding commission of the offense. Within each of these categories certain major and minor themes are stressed.

Life History: The Role of Work, Family, and Community Life

Some combination of family, work, and community contribution are thought by most judges to be relevant to the assessment of the defendant, though these factors are rarely dispositive. Often, as in the first two quotations to follow, a prior good record gets weight but does not overcome the seriousness of the defendant's conduct or his failure to show an appropriately remorseful attitude:

[Sentencing of a securities fraud defendant guilty of many counts]: One of the people had a really unblemished record. But he was in the ____right up to his ears. He was doing all kinds of terrible things. He was an officer in the National Guard, serving active duty, getting paid teaching ROTC kids. He was a West Point graduate, became a stockbroker, and he became one of the worst thieves on Wall Street. His family was exemplary, he was well regarded in the community. We had letters at sentencing from everybody and his brother. But the guy was really—his depredations, he was really just about as fraudulent as a fellow could be.

In this situation, I had a corporation president before me. . . . The defendant had an exemplary personal history. He had been a high performance executive in several major corporations. He had a long list of organizational associations in his community. He had three children, a very good family life. And here he was essentially embezzling funds from this company to support personal adventures in the stock market and personal luxuries. [The judge reports that this defendant's prior personal background would have gotten him probation, but he failed to show sorrow and remorse for his offense, and he also was not honest about the money after being caught.]

But sometimes the combination of past good deeds and present circumstances can cut the other way:

[Discussing a sales manager, a very modest man who had never been in trouble before] who miraculously in my judgment having raised four youngsters is succeeding in helping his four kids go to college. He had completed two college educations [for his children] and was in the middle of a third one and another one coming along. I think that at the end of the trial he was probably ticketed for a year, maybe eighteen months. But when I learned this about him, he did have a job, a good one, a good, solid job in Atlanta, Georgia, when this whole thing came out. I checked with the Bureau of Prisons and found that the only work-release program which was available in Atlanta was no more than six months. . . . So he ends up with six months' work-release.

Life History: The Role of Personal Characteristics

Along with work, family, and community contributions judges are often interested in making an assessment of personal attributes. We have already noted one personal attribute, namely, a good war record, that is sometimes mentioned by judges as deserving weight in their decision. Another attribute is IQ: "I guess my feeling was that this man was a real prey on society. He was bright. If he turned his mind to noncriminal activities he could be—with the brilliance he used in criminal activity, he probably would have done very well." Indeed, sentencing of white-collar defendants may be one arena in social life where the intellectually disadvantaged get a break: [Explaining why one of two defendants got probation in a cattle fraud case]: "The second person was not too bright; he was sucked into the illegal scheme. . . . He was a decent, hard-working kid."

Often factors relating to health and age get added into the equation, although they have a logically more important role in assessing the consequences of sanctioning, as we shall see in chapter 5. We give two examples here to show how judges are likely to add elements from rather different domains into their overall judgment in sentence:

> [Sentencing a woman who had previously stolen from a doctor and received a term sentence]: She really should have received the statutory maximum except that her health was very poor. She has a lot of family responsibilities, children and the like.

> [Speaking of sentencing a Watergate-related figure]: He had an exemplary record of community service, exemplary family life. He was an elderly man, an old man. Nothing useful would be served by a jail sentence.

The Dilemma of Praiseworthy Conduct and Blameworthy Status

One of the most difficult tasks for judges is to find the proper balance in assessing the generally praiseworthy past conduct of many white-collar defendants while at the same time taking into account that their greater advantage and social position in life may impose a special obligation on them to obey the law. A great many of the judges' comments deal with this dilemma. Thus:

> The possibilities that a white-collar criminal is going to have done some good service to the community in the past is certainly more likely to be present than with your street criminal.

... They have good backgrounds in a sense that they have achieved some things, they have contributed something to society. ...

In a white-collar case I'm often dealing with someone ... who comes in with a packet of all kinds of positive information on his background, ministers' letters, public officials' letters. ... The decision is definitely tougher.

But equally impressive arguments go the other way. One judge noted that a factor in common crime defendants is frequently a broken home:

Now I don't think that society has to put up indefinitely with the behavior of somebody just because he had an unhappy childhood. On the other hand, from the humanistic standpoint, when you read the childhood and backgrounds of many of these offenders, you can see that their ultimate course was determined before they were old enough to make decisions for themselves. And when that happens it has an impact upon the sentence.

Another judge talked about the

poor slobs who come into this court and who have not had some of the privileges the white-collar criminals have, and who are in a mess because the system is working against them. [He has to balance that off against the greater hope for the one with more resources.]

Another judge made the point more generally:

There is a philosophy that it is terribly unfair, where they have had all of the advantages in life where the others have not, that they not be punished severely.

The nature of the dilemma is perhaps best portrayed in the following extended quotation from one of our judges:

I don't think they [the white-collar crime cases] are any more troublesome to the judge in performing the function, but I think that they have a peculiar characteristic to them which is perhaps more challenging to a judge as to what a proper sentence is. I don't think we agonize over them any more than we do over the other kinds of cases and the imposition of sentencing in other kinds of cases.

But I think we do have this situation, and this as I see it is the nub of the matter in the imposition of sentences in so-called white-collar cases. Usually the defendant is one who looks as though he can resume his place, if indeed not just continue on in his place in society, as a valuable and contributing member of society. Almost always hc is a husband and a father. Almost always he has children who are in the process of becoming what we like to think children ought to be—well brought up, well educated, nurtured, cared for. Usually he is a member of the kinds of civic organizations in the community who value his services and derive value from his services. In other words, if you are thinking in terms of rehabilitation as a purpose to be achieved in the imposition of sentences, the odds greatly favor the rehabilitation of a so-called white-collar criminal than they do in any other, almost inherently so. As a result you are up against this more difficult problem in degree in the so-called white-collar criminals as to whether you are not going to inflict a hurt on society by putting such a person in a prison and making him cease to be a good father and a good husband and a good worker in the community.

And of course, then counterbalanced against that is this business of whether there isn't typically a greater abuse of trust of some kind that is involved in the crime committed by the white-collar criminal. So you do have, it seems to me, typically in white-collar crimes for sentence purposes a different set of countervailing interests. Different at least in degree, if not in kind, from what you do—the bank robber is typically from the lowest strata of society measured by his education or his family background, his general position in the community. The community very seldom suffers from taking such a person out of the street or off the street. He needs to be made something that he isn't. And as a result, the imposition of sentence is frequently more readily recognizable as a contribution toward his benefit and society than it is in the white-collar crimes. The only factor in the white-collar crime that sometimes looms so large and heavily is that if some fellow who has derived all the benefits that our society has to offer is allowed to get away with a high crime and escape with a lesser penalty than the person of lesser status, there is almost inherently therc, some suggestion at least, of unfairness. And that has to be a factor.

High status is thus generally associated with a variety of attributes that would, in and of themselves, justify viewing the criminal offense as an isolated event. At the same time many judges do not want to reward offenders simply because of their social advantages. They feel that the commission of a crime by persons who have had all of life's advantage is, in many ways, particularly serious. It is a kind of waste of those advantages, and it deprives white-collar offenders of one prominent excuse, namely, prior personal deprivation. However, as we will see in chapter 5, it may serve, at the same time, as another kind of argument for mitigation.

Judicial Assessments of Motive

In his book *Other People's Money*, a study of persons who violate financial trust, Donald R. Cressey dealt at length with the offenders' vocabularies of motive—the language they used to explain to themselves and others how they could have done what they did.[29] Like the defendants themselves, judges often feel that an assessment of the defendant's motives for the offense is an essential ingredient in coming to a clear picture of their blameworthiness. The situational nature of the needs and problems facing some defendants served to separate their cases, in the minds of judges, from others who commit crimes because they are psychopathic personalities or career crooks.

The most common way features of motive enter into the discussion is through the need vs. greed distinction—those who have a clear economic need for money and those who operate out of motives of greed. Consider the following exchange:

> INTERVIEWER: What about a corporate director who is embezzling or skimming or whatever, causing serious financial damage to stockholders and the public? . . . Obviously he has no criminal background, not been arrested before, outstanding person in his community, a member of charitable organizations, exemplary family life, but he is doing, for whatever reason, he is caught in a situation in the business community where he is clearly violating some basic standard of corporate behavior.
>
> JUDGE: You say that there are reasons for his doing it? Is he strapped for money? Does he just take it with the intention of

29. Dryden Press, 1953.

returning it, but just happens to be caught at the time? Now he has lost his job, now he is driving a truck, he has got four kids he is supporting. Send him to jail? No, not that one. But the president of the corporation who is motivated by greed alone and is with a scheme, a plan, milking the company, he has got to go to jail. . . . He is criminally oriented to begin with, and to allow this man to serve straight probation would be mocking justice.

The same judge discussed one of his own real cases:

[The defendant] was a vice-president of a bank. He had a business making hair pieces. He found himself in a financial bind, and in order to salvage this business, he borrowed some money. He juggled the books, fully intending to pay it back. He was caught, came in, guilty, asked him why, was contrite, was willing to accept any punishment the court meted out, driving a truck—the vice-president of a bank driving a truck—poor. I think the oldest child was something like fourteen years of age. This man will never commit that same crime. First of all he will never have the opportunity again, and he wasn't really motivated to perform a criminal act. In his mind he was borrowing money at the time. I really believed him. I gave him straight probation.

Another judge contrasted situational temptation with greed:

The guy who has some business problems and just needs some money and takes it. He doesn't intend to deprive his employer of that money. He fully intends to return it. It just so happens that he took it at the wrong time and he is caught. . . . But in an income tax evasion case I had, the defendants were out and out guilty and intended to cheat the government of taxes. Greed motivated them.

Another judge, sitting in a western jurisdiction, spoke to the need/greed distinction in a slightly different manner. Referring to a securities or mail fraud case (the judge was uncertain about which statute controlled, but he gave the defendant five years), he said,

This guy was a small, "marginal con man." What I mean by con man is someone who consciously set out to mislead people and does that as a profession. It is not that he is involved in a legitimate business and somehow oversteps the boundary. A con man's very business purpose is illegitimate. Anyway this guy was a marginal con man. . . . This wasn't a crime that could be explained by this defendant's own difficult situation, his need or poverty like what goes on with some of these bank tellers. This was outright greed and complete disregard of the common person, the little old lady who invested all her savings, the elderly couple, hundreds upon hundreds of them.

Later in the interview he contrasted this case involving land fraud with another case

which is very much not like the land fraud case although it is a fraud case. It is the bank teller who embezzles. These are middle-class and lower-middle-class people who are up to their ears in debt. The money they work with in the bank begins to look just like pieces of paper. They are trying to pay off a mortgage and a loan and they just can't resist the temptation. I usually sentence these people to a term of probation and no more and probably require that they make restitution if they possibly can.

The judge went on to distinguish this case from the disregard for human lives shown in the land fraud case, where the defendant is

just as bad as one who uses violence. These land fraud cases in which thousands of people have gotten hurt, who have lost their total life savings, they are perpetrated by people who are just like the guys who hit you over the head.

Another judge contrasted the case of "an ex-lawyer out of Chicago who had been disbarred" and a securities agent. He had given the ex-lawyer two consecutive sentences of three years each and the securities agent a far lesser sentence. Here assessment of blameworthiness involves a judgment about whether the crime was an isolated event or part of a continuing pattern of behavior. Note how the judge constructed a "prior record" for the ex-lawyer and saw the securities agent as a first offender. He explained the difference:

You could see here I felt that the person [the ex-lawyer] was a professional criminal. This was a man who was making his livelihood over a long period of time by fraudulently exploiting people who don't know any better. This is a different type of person than my securities agent. One has to take into account that securities agents and others in business who are more and more exposed to temptations of business, temptations which can draw one easily over the line where legal acts quickly begin to become technically illegal, but are still part of general business practices. I don't condone this type of thing. But it is not the same thing as when one is dealing with a real bunko man. The real con man is going to be a con man from day one until he dies. This securities agent wasn't this type of person. He was remorseful. He showed tremendous concern. I assume that he saw it as an opportunity for a fast buck. I would say, "He slipped and fell." The difference here is one between the salesman's puff and illegality, and real crime.

Another type of case sometimes provides the judge with a defendant whose motives for crime may have been partly altruistic:

There is a difference between a motive to—you know a businessman is desperately trying to save a dying business so his employees won't get fired and so forth. He may commit a crime but the degree of moral culpability is different from another fellow who is just—well the extreme would be if someone is just interested in milking the company and taking all the cash out of it and that is all he is ever doing anyway.

Although perhaps the most frequent contrast concerning need and greed is between the businessman whose enterprise is failing and the true con man, the more personal side of family finances may also be present—the person of limited income who is sending several children to college, for example. One judge noted that in sentencing a public figure, one with a long and distinguished record, for bribery, he had to give him a severe sentence because there were no such redeeming or justifying contingencies: "Well, suppose a person with a long public record and very exemplary life and what not, had a wife who was terribly ill and he couldn't pay his hospital bills, and he stole. That would be a different position, a different situation. I would give a very different consideration to that."

Even as judges assess motives and use their assessments in determining the appropriate sanction, they are not unaware of the fact that they might on occasion be misled, and, as we shall see later, they respond especially strongly if they feel that the defendants have lied to them or misled them, whether or not it takes the form of perjury in their courtroom. They do, nevertheless, rely on commonsense moral judgments of motive to distinguish sharply between defendants who, in other respects, might be seen as quite similar.

Assessing Blameworthiness: Evidence from Words and Deeds during the Process of Trial, Conviction, and Sentencing

Just as the judges look backward in time from the offense itself to the motives or the prior moral careers of offenders, so they look forward from the crime to the defendant's actions and words while moving through the criminal process. Indeed, it is striking how often judgments of the defendant's blameworthiness are based not on involvement in the crime itself but on assessments of character and behavior based on events occurring months and sometimes years after the offending behavior for which the defendant is convicted. Although these assessments, or perhaps reassessments, take a great many different forms, they fall into three basic clusters: First, judges are particularly concerned about defendants who try to cover up their offenses and especially those who do so on the stand by lying. Second, the judges are concerned that defendants exhibit remorse or contrition for their offenses, or at least indicate a capacity to accept blame for their misdeeds. Third, judges give substantial weight to defendants' cooperation with government officials, especially when it is stressed by prosecutors.

On Lying and Cover-up

In chapter 2 we discussed the many ways in which judges get information about offenders. There we described the way in which judges use trials as vehicles to get a picture of the offense and the offender. One of the ways that picture is filled in is through an assessment of the defendant's credibility on the witness stand. Judges are very attentive to defendants' testimony as well as to the way they present themselves when they testify in their own defense. If their testimony contradicts the preponderance of evidence, judges often conclude that the defendant is lying. Lying on the stand is not only a criminal offense in and of itself, but it provides the judges with an important indicator of the offender's character. As one judge described a defendant in a complicated fraud case,

JUDGE: The case went to trial, and he was convicted.

INTERVIEWER: Did the defendant take the stand?

JUDGE: Yes he did, and he lied. That was my view of him at least.

INTERVIEWER: What impression did you get of him as an individual person—let me ask the question a different way: Did the impression you get of him affect your sentencing consideration, and if so, what was that impression?

JUDGE: Yes, it did. As you know . . . this is an area of great debate, and you run into the cases which say that the sentencing judge cannot increase the sentence he has imposed in a particular case just because perjury was committed by the defendant in the course of the trial. He is not there for sentence for perjury. And they also say that you can't in effect deprive one of his constitutional right to testify on his own behalf if he wishes to do so by penalizing him for having done so. Well those all run counter to the fact that the sentencing judge has a prime desire and need to know that defendant just as well as he can. And one of the ways that you come to know him is by his performance on the witness stand. If it also happens to be perjury, so be it. But you get a reading on the kind of person he is.

Many of the judges with whom we spoke clearly related lying on the stand to a more severe sentence. As one judge put it in describing his sentence in a securities fraud case,

I might say that I tend to give out slightly longer sentences to people who try to obstruct the determination of guilt by either lying or misleading the court, not just by going to trial but this was a case where one of the reasons that two of them got as much as a year was that I thought both of them had lied on the witness stand. And I count that against people.

Or, as another judge said, "And often with a person who testifies I get a view that he is lying. I do get that view and in respect to it I get hard."

Lying on the stand is, according to our judges, often part of a continuing pattern or effort to cover up an offense. As one judge put it, when a defendant lies on the stand—tries to do "a snow job on me"—he is just continuing the behavior that got him in trouble in the first place. Another argued that white-collar criminals tended to be "practiced liars": "They start out lying about their tax liabilities or business practices; they get caught and give 'excuses' or reasons for committing a crime that are simply not true to the investigators. They lie to their lawyer as a way of 'saving face' and then they lie in court." All of this is, in the judge's view, "an attempt, if you will, to continue the crime."

Words used by judges to describe their reaction to a defendant who lies in court ranged from "put out" and "annoyed" to "angry" and "indignant." But there is more than just emotions involved in explaining the effect of such lying on the sentence. Two themes stand out. First, the defendant who lies on the stand, in effect, undermines the defense effort to portray him, either during the trial or the sentencing phase, as an upstanding person of good character. This removes what is, in many cases, an important argument in favor of judicial leniency. Second, the defendant who lies on the stand is perceived to be unrepentant. He is someone for whom arrest and prosecution have meant little or nothing. As one judge put it in talking about representations made to him by the defendant in a tax case,

> I found on reexamination that there was an attempt being made to mislead me as to the seriousness of the man's illness. And where I had been sympathetic I must say I have found that the facts as represented were not true. The man had misrepresented the state of his health. And when I took that on balance, I remember I sentenced that particular white-collar defendant to a four-year term because I thought that not only had he not learned from his initial activity but he, using the word again, exacerbated the offense by trying to fool me and it is bad enough to try to fool a judge but if it turns out that the attempt is unsuccessful, I think you have a judge who feels that not only has the man not learned from his experience but as a matter of fact he is continuing the same dishonest activity. Therefore, an appropriate sentence would be a moderate period of confinement, probably more than I would have given in the first instance had I not learned that there was an attempt to mislead me, to gain my sympathy on grounds of poor health. And it turned out that this was an exaggerated situation which was done by the defendant for my benefit. And that resulted ultimately in my determining that in light of what this particular man had done and what he had done afterwards a four-year sentence was appropriate.

In the end judges seem to take such continuing misbehavior as a good indicator of the kind of person they are dealing with. Offenders who lie during the criminal process are "particularly unpleasant characters" and "thoroughly lousy fellows."

On Expressions of Remorse and Contrition

In addition to truthfulness, it is important for many judges that defendants recognize the gravity of their offense, accept the blame for their misdeeds, and express remorse or contrition for them. Sometimes this judgment is joined with judgments of candor in a kind of global assessment of the defendant. For example, one judge explained his reading of the pre-sentence investigation as follows:

> I look at . . . the official version [and] the defendant's version . . . And sometimes I reach a conclusion where I think he is being totally false or if not totally false he is covering up. I think that creates in my mind a reaction to the extent that remorse and contrition in the sense of "I've been caught this time and I better not do it again"— then if I reach a conclusion that a fellow is really not being truthful, I have that in my mind.

Another judge explained his sentence of a prison term for a corporate president with an exemplary personal history:

> INTERVIEWER: From what you said earlier, I would have thought that this person would have received a probation sentence. He had that exemplary background, etc.
>
> JUDGE: He would have except for the fact that he perjured himself and he didn't show any remorse. I think he would have had a probation disposition if it hadn't been for his failure to show sorrow and remorse for what he had done. He just didn't seem sorry and there was the issue where the money was going. If he had been sorry and if he had told the truth about the—where the money was going, I am sure he would have had a probation disposition.

Often judgments of remorse stand more on their own. In a case involving a conspiracy to defraud record companies, the judge noted that the pre-sentence investigation report indicated that there was real remorse. Real remorse, he indicated, was common in white-collar cases and weighed heavily with him.

If failure to show remorse adds to blameworthiness, even more so does the effort to shift blame from one party to another. Note how one judge explained the severity of his sentence of a seventy-year-old industrialist convicted of a large embezzlement.

> What really turned the tide against him was that, although he pleaded guilty, he attempted to put most of the blame for it on his brother, who was by that time deceased and really couldn't speak for himself. The indications were that while his brother may have incidentally profited from what he was doing, that he was the moving party of these embezzlements. I gave him a year in jail despite his age and illness.

Sometimes the heart of the expression is not so much one of remorse, but of recognition of the utterly foolish or stupid nature of the act in question:

> I have a fellow, for example, that will be brought in here who cheated on his income tax return. He put in a $250 deduction for hospital expenses or doctor expenses. In fact it was $25 and it was audited. He altered the check, a $25 check into a $250 check. And this will be a fellow, for example, whose income is around $50,000 a year. Now that fellow is an utter fool to have done that, and I am typically impressed with the fact that he recognizes that by the time of sentencing that he was. I think I recognize him as a fellow who is not likely to do anything criminal again.

Some judges noted that remorse and contrition count in all kinds of cases, not just white-collar cases. But they count more in cases for defendants without a prior record:

> If a person is contrite and admits what he has done, he is less likely to get a prison sentence. I might say that is true of blue-collar crime also, if the fellow has no prior record. If a person has a prior record, you have a right to assume that his protestations are not sincere.

The subtle nature of the judgment and the danger of being misled in fact were mentioned by a number of judges. These views were given expression by a judge explaining his attitude toward a stockbroker who was a defendant in a counterfeit stock case and who pleaded guilty:

I think in this individual's case the plea of guilty represented a tactical awareness of the evidence against him. He pleaded guilty on the advice of his attorneys, who gave him the only advice that they could in the circumstances. But this man still couldn't quite see it. Now he didn't go quite so far as to say "I didn't do anything wrong." He could have said that and still have a constitutional plea of guilty accepted under *North Carolina v. Alford*, if the judge is satisfied on the basis of the allocution and any further inquiries that he might make that there is indeed a factual basis for the plea. We didn't quite have that situation here, but the man did not have, it seemed to me, what I would regard as an appropriate awareness of the nature of what he had done. Now I mention that as a factor. I think looking back on it it was a factor in my thinking. I don't think it was of relatively greater significance.

The judge continued,

I think it is proper for judges to draw a distinction between the immediate plea and genuinely repentant criminal and the defiant or sullen or grudging one. If you give too much consideration to it then you are a sitting duck, I suppose, for sham protestations of remorse and breast-beating, and buckets of tears and appeals of sympathy. And you have got to watch out for that and part of the sentencing process is invariably making a value judgment on the genuineness of the appeals you receive, both from the defendant, expressions of contrition or remorse, and from the people who write in for him. And I have no doubt that some are more genuine than others, but you have got to do the best you can to evaluate those. To the extent that I feel I am able to distinguish between the genuinely repentant and the defiant defendant, I will give it some consideration.

INTERVIEWER: In this particular case, there was an allocution and the defendant didn't simply express a genuine sense of remorse?

JUDGE: That is right. He was saying, in effect, "Well maybe you have got me technically. But I really don't think what I did was so bad if indeed it was even bad at all." Well, technically they have him nailed to the wall . . . , at the center of participation in a rather substantial fraudulent scheme, and I did not find that attitude particularly appealing.

On Cooperation

While judgments of remorse and contrition depend heavily upon the words and the appearance of the defendant, judgments of cooperation depend more heavily upon deeds. Whether cooperative acts are taken as signs of repentance and reform or are simply rewarded because they help criminal justice operatives, those who cooperate with government officials are likely to get a break at the time of sentencing. The centrality of cooperation is suggested in the following exchange:

> INTERVIEWER: What is it about—let's say an income tax evader, or someone who engages in postal embezzlement, what would be in their background that would lean you toward leniency? What are some of the considerations that might push you in a more lenient direction in sentencing?
>
> JUDGE: One, they might help catch a lot of other rascals. That would help.

Another judge noted that he seldom accepts recommendations for sentence, but that one area where he is likely to follow the sentence recommendation made by the prosecutor is where the defendant cooperates. These judgments clearly put the judge in a dependent position, vis-à-vis the prosecution. One judge put it as follows:

> I am sure that some people will cooperate, not very effectively. Others do so. And of course the judge has to rely on what the government tells him about the extent of cooperation. You seldom have a chance to really assess it objectively. . . . Usually what the government will do is at the request of the defendant, will tell me, Mr. John Doe testified in the X case for the government, and so far as we can tell his testimony was fruitful and the defendant was convicted. In this case [a securities fraud with eight defendants] there was a two-page letter which went into his cooperation in great detail, cooperation that lead to the discovery of other crimes. It was an enthusiastic letter that didn't come up with any recommendation at the end, but it was perfectly clear that they hoped I would get the point. It was an unusual letter. . . . I guess the government pros-

ecutors would be pretty much out of business if they didn't have informers.

The importance of the judge's role in validating the prosecutor's efforts to get cooperation is evidenced in the following extended account:

I think that the heart and soul of the plea bargaining between the prosecutor and the defendant in a case like this, and particularly with reference to someone who is then going to testify either before a petty jury on a trial against others, or to assist a grand jury to continue the investigation, is that when the individual who has pleaded guilty comes on before the judge for sentencing, the prosecutor is going to say that this man has been very helpful to us. That is the real incentive in this kind of situation. It is not so much, I think, to get rid of three additional counts upon which the judge can sentence you. It is to have an opportunity to impress the prosecutor with your remorse, repentance or whatever—the value of your cooperation—and have the prosecutor say so to the judge. It will make a difference to the judge I think. At least it does to me.

I am aware that it is necessary for the U.S. Attorney's Office to have this kind of cooperation if it is going to go after other people who should be gone after. And it is important, or it is a factor which should be considered, that the U.S. Attorney's Office should be in a position to say in like comparable cases that arise in the future, if you cooperate we can't promise you anything but it is the sort of thing which very well might do you some good. They can't very well say that unless judges take into consideration and react to the prosecutor's representation that there has been meaningful and helpful cooperation.

Despite its importance, some judges are aware that there is a limit to the reward one can get from cooperating. One judge put it as follows:

When pleas of guilty come in, [and there is] a rehabilitative sense of saying yes, I did it, I'm caught, I give up, entitles a person to consideration, but with me not exoneration, and similarly the fact that when caught he describes the complicity of others and that entitles him to consideration, but not exoneration either. I am not satisfied that the society is properly served because when caught somebody says yeah, that is the fellow who helped me.

Finally, the fusion of contrition and cooperation is suggested in this judge's account of the sentencing of a man who pled guilty in a stock fraud case:

> I sentenced the fellow who pleaded guilty a couple of weeks ago, and the assistant U.S. attorney very properly said that in his experience, which was considerable, he had never seen an individual who was (a) more promptly and genuinely repentant, and (b) as a token and evidence of that repentance, (and perhaps also wanting to save his own skin even though those are frequently confused) but the prosecutor said that he was very, very helpful to him, that he had been right from the start, both before the grand jury and on the trial, and he regarded the cooperation as quite essential to the successful prosecution of a considerably greater villian, and I paid attention to that.
>
> The choice was whether or not in a substantial fraud, he should be imprisoned or admitted to probation. And I put him on probation. He had no prior criminal record, no violence, "victimless" crimes. And so those factors rather incline me toward probation. But the clincher was in fact that the prosecutor was able to say that he had been very, very helpful and I think you have got to encourage that. Not that it becomes the decisive factor, no single factor should be decisive but it is an important factor.

Every convicted defendant is blameworthy in the narrow sense that he or she has been shown to have the requisite mental state for the commission of a crime, that is, to be criminally responsible. But that showing provides the barest beginnings of a judge's wrestling with the moral character of a defendant. The judges we interviewed considered a wide variety of acts and mental states as morally significant, enabling them to make substantial and refined distinctions between offenders who might appear quite similar if one looked only at the legal wrong committed and the harm it caused.

A portrait of the least blameworthy among defendants would look like this: the defendant showed little deliberateness, calculation, or scheming in the commission of the offense; if others were involved in the offense, the defendant played only a minor role and was not central either to the planning or to the conduct of the offense. The defendant's prior life has been led in an orderly, upright fashion and includes contributions to family, work, and community life. The defendant's motive for the offense was need rather than greed and especially a need to help others. The defendant was candid about the offense and his role in it and honest and forthright in all his dealings with the judge. The defendant accepted responsibility for the offense and showed remorse and contrition for what damage the offense may have caused. And the defendant cooperated fully with government agents in any other matters pertaining to this case and related ones. The most blameworthy defendants will be at the opposite end of the spectrum on each of these qualities.

We are not arguing that all judges agree with this vision of the elements of blameworthiness. Clearly they attach greater or lesser weight to the various qualities, a topic we treat in chapter 6. But we do believe, matters of relative weighting aside, that there is broad agreement among the judges that these are the kinds of qualities that should count in making an assessment of the defendant's moral career and that such an assessment is relevant to the sentence to be meted out. While we defer until our final chapter the value and policy questions this portrait raises, if we have fairly described the broad central tendency of federal district court judges with respect to assessments of blameworthiness, the question still remains: Is it appropriate that all these elements come into play? Do we want a system in which judges engage in moral reconstructions of defendants' prior careers? Or would we prefer, as some guidelines systems have it, to restrict judges' considerations of background features to those of demonstrated criminal record, rather than allowing them to use biographical data to construct subtle and refined, though arguably unreliable judgments of character?

The attributes of blameworthiness bear an interesting relationship to the formal legal structure. The only attribute that is clearly and centrally implicated in the formal criminal law is that of intention, or deliberateness, which forms part of the core legal notion of criminal responsibility. That notion has much to say about the qualities of the mind at and immediately preceding the time of the crime in question. But many of the attributes of blameworthiness judges work with are at a far remove from the offense itself, lying either much earlier in the defendant's life or far later, in his attitudes and actions during the phases of indictment and conviction up to sentencing. Many of these attributes are seemingly more in keeping with the notion of individualized determinations of sentencing under a now nearly abandoned rehabilitative ideal, when each defendant's unique individuality was to be given expression in the sentence, than under the recently rediscovered "just deserts" model of sentencing.

The attributes of harm discussed in chapter 3 and those of blameworthiness described in chapter 4 bear an intimate relationship to one another. As we noted at the end of chapter 3, the concept of trust and its violation seems to us to be a key link between them. Trust violations are serious offenses in and of themselves, often bringing grave damage to the fabric of community life. They also speak to the moral character of those who commit them, placing them in a more blameworthy category than those who do not occupy positions of moral responsibility and trust.

As we noted at the beginning of chapter 3, there is a basic link among all the concepts dealt with in these two chapters. When the judges talk about their work they are most likely to speak, not in terms of offenders or offenses, but in terms of "cases," which represent a combination of the two. Many of our interviews contained assertions like, "The other day I had a case that . . . " and most often the judge would proceed to describe attributes both of offense and of offender. We have articulated them separately in these two chapters and have preserved the analytical distinction between act and actor, because judges sometimes do talk about them in separate terms and because the attributes they stress are naturally different, one set being appropriate to judgments of harm, the other to those of blameworthiness. But in judges' work these two are likely to fuse into judgments about the seriousness of a case.

The attributes of harm and of blameworthiness come together to allow an overall judgment of the seriousness of a case, and the elements of those judgments, the elements laid out in chapters 3 and 4, provide a kind of common law of sentencing with respect to white-collar offenders. It is not to be found in any casebook or in any sentencing manual, but it is articulated in a variety of ways by federal judges as they discuss the task of sentencing. Finally, although many other considerations come into play as a judge arrives at a sentence, we believe these twin concepts of harm and blameworthiness, fused into an overall judgment of the seriousness of a case, form a kind of bedrock or anchoring point against which the other considerations must work their influence if they are to have an effect.

■ 5

Assessing the Consequences
of the Sentence

*Upon the principle of utility, it [punishment] ought
to be admitted in as far as it promises to exclude
some greater evil.*— Bentham, An Introduction to
the Principles of Morals and Legislation

Sentencing decisions are firmly anchored in the judge's rethinking
through and further specification of the two major considerations that
underlie the criminal law: concern for the harm caused by the offense
and for the culpability of the offender. Judges develop, in effect,
expanded concepts of harm and blameworthiness that enable them to
consider variables and circumstances not built into the statute law or
the common law, but that are close cousins of the underlying values
reflected in that law.

But important as these are, they are not all the judges are doing.
Judges are also working within a framework that gives specific room
for consequence—for examining the sentence not as an expression of
value judgments about harm and blameworthiness, but as a means of
giving effect to policies that have their roots in utilitarian thinking.
These policies are many, but two of them predominate in the thinking
of federal judges about white-collar crime sentencing. The first is a
concern for the effect of the sentence on some broader audience—
sometimes as broad as the whole society, other times only as broad
as persons in the offender's situation who might be tempted to engage
in crime themselves. The second set of policies is concerned with the
effect on the offender, or those in his immediate environment.[1]

In this chapter we review the judges' thinking with respect to the

---

1. There is an important sense in which the concept of desert, as reflected in
the combination of harm and blameworthiness, does itself have a crucial consequence, namely, that of limiting the range of permissible sanctions otherwise justified under a utilitarian rationale. Judges find it difficult to consider a sanction for
deterrent purposes that is not also deserved on grounds of harm and blame. In
this sense it would be wrong to think of desert as looking only to the past and
deterrence to the future, for the latter is itself constrained by the former.

relevance of each of these considerations. Before doing so, however, we discuss the emergence of consequence—or policy oriented thinking—as a core legal norm in its own right.

The Emergence of Consequence as a Core Legal Norm

Unlike the development of the concepts of harm and blameworthiness, the emergence of systematic thinking about consequence in Anglo-American legal thought need be traced no further back than the eighteenth century.[2] We have already described (in chapter 3) the beginning of the legal reforms in England and on the Continent that led to a reexamination of the extreme penalties for many crimes and a strong pressure to make the sentences for crime proportional to the harm done. A critical ingredient in this shift was the doctrine of utilitarianism as it came to be expressed by Jeremy Bentham, who in turn had been influenced by Beccaria.

While much of the concern of those interested in the grading of offenses was to insure that an appropriate level of moral condemnation would be visited on those who committed the offense in question,[3]

2. During the eighteenth century a marked change in thinking about the criminal law spread throughout England, with its motive force the writings and public speaking of the utilitarians in England. Dicey describes the period immediately preceding the utilitarian reform movement in England as one of "quiescence," in which "[t]he laws were antiquated, the statute book . . . defaced by enactments condemned by the humane feeling of later times" (Albert Venn Dicey, *Lectures on the Relation between Law and Public Opinion during the Nineteenth Century* [London: Macmillan, 1905], 79). This period of quiescence seems to have come to an end by the middle of the nineteenth century, when a great reform movement began to show its results in new legislation and in a growing attitude in the English bar that law could be an instrument of change for the betterment of the general social condition. The new era is labeled by Dicey as Benthamite liberalism: "The name of one man, it is true, can never adequately summarise a whole school of thought, but from 1825 onwards the teaching of Bentham (1748–1832) exercised so potent an influence that to him is fairly ascribed that thoroughgoing though gradual amendment of the law of England" (ibid., 125).

3. Pollock and Maitland find vengeance rooted deeply in the early sources of law, English as well as other, and whatever came after it as a new or different rationale of punishment; there is no question that revenge has remained prominent in legal thought as a prime justification for the criminal law. Of what they called the ancient system, Pollock and Maitland gave a frightening account:

evidence which comes to us from England and elsewhere invites us to think of utilitarians had a different agenda. Utilitarianism is truly the intellectual progenitor of consequential thinking in Anglo-American jurisprudence; it is thus instructive to chart its beginnings because it constitutes such a distinctive part of the legal culture American judges work in and draw from.

At its most basic level, utilitarianism is a theory of human behavior. It says that men act for no other reason than to achieve pleasure and avoid pain, a theory simple in its formulation but revolutionary in its negation of supernatural and moral concepts of human behavior. The famous formula "the greatest happiness of the greatest number" springs from a concept of man as hedonistic and rational in his choice of pleasure-producing goals. Says Bentham, "Nature has placed mankind under the governance of two sovereign masters, pain and pleasure. It is for them alone to point out what we ought to do as well as to determine what we shall do."[4]

Out of this curt description of human nature grows a theory of government in which the state can manipulate pain and pleasure to achieve the social order of the greatest good. In Bentham's main work, *An Introduction to the Principles of Morals and Legislation*, the criminal law stands as a primary vehicle of the state to achieve the desired

---

a time when law was weak, and its weakness was displayed by a ready recourse to outlawry. It could not measure its blows; he who defined it was outside its sphere; he was outlaw. He who breaks the law has gone to war with the community; the community goes to war with him. It is the right and duty of every man to pursue him, to ravage his land, to burn his house, to hunt him down like a wild beast and slay him; for a wild beast he is; not merely is he a 'friendless man,' he is a wolf (Sir Frederick Pollock and Frederic William Maitland, *The History of English Law before the Time of Edward I*, 2d ed. [Cambridge: Cambridge University Press, 1968], 449).

And in 1883 the distinguished historian Stephen wrote as follows about the criminal law:

infliction of punishment by law gives definite expression and a solenm ratification and justification to the hatred which is excited by the commission of the offence, and which constitutes the moral or popular as distinguished from the conscientious sanction of that part of morality which is also sanctioned by the criminal law. The criminal law thus proceeds upon the principle that it is morally right to hate criminals, and it confirms and justifies that sentiment by inflicting upon criminals punishments which express it (Sir James Fitzjames Stephen, *A History of the Criminal Law of England* [London: Macmillan, 1883], 81–82).

4. *An Introduction to the Principles of Morals and Legislation* (Oxford: Clarendon Press, 1879), 1.

consequences of communal betterment. "The business of government," said Bentham,

> is to promote the happiness of the society, by punishing and rewarding. That part of its business which consists in punishing, is more particularly the subject of penal law. In proportion as an act tends to disturb that happiness, in proportion as the tendency of it is pernicious, will be the demand it creates for punishment.[5]

This essential identity of acts and punishments—both tied to the central notion of consequence—is also prominent in Bentham's introductory chapter on punishment: "The general object which all laws have . . . is . . . to exclude mischief. But all punishment is mischief; all punishment in itself is evil. Upon the principle of utility, if it ought at all to be admitted, it ought to be admitted in as far as it promises to exclude some greater evil."[6] Bentham's first rule of punishment follows directly from this juxtaposition of punishment and happiness: "The value of the punishment must not be less in any case than what is sufficient to out weigh that of the profit of the offense."[7] This is a complete deterrence theory in which the measure of the punishment is linked to the measure of profits from the crime.

Such a theory creates a radical shift in our thinking about crime. The punishment was to be set at a level that would take the profit out of the offense. Penalties will depend not on a moral judgment about the gravity of harm or the culpability of the offender, but on a strategic judgment about the amount of pain necessary to deter the criminal from seeking the profits of the crime.

There is no question that Bentham had a profound effect on Amer-

5. Ibid., 71.
6. Ibid., 70.
7. The social good was supposed to be defined, according to Bentham, in terms of acts and their potential to produce happiness. This formula made the notion of consequence paramount. "The general tendency of an act is more or less pernicious," said Bentham, "according to the sum total of its *consequences*: that is, according to the difference between the sum of such as are good, and the sum of such as are evil" (ibid.) (emphasis added). The philosophical point of this equation was that every act should be interpreted in light of its consequences. And what was important about consequences could only be whether they caused pain or pleasure: "Now among the consequences of an act, be they what they may, such only . . . can be said to be material, as either consist of pain or pleasure, or have an influence in the production of pain or pleasure" (ibid.).

ican legal thought, both to laissez-faire philosophy[8] and to the emerging ideas of the welfare state.[9] Fitting the punishment to the profit is the cornerstone of deterrence theory in Anglo-American jurisprudence. One link between Bentham and American legal theory is the work of Holmes:

> there can be no case in which the law-maker makes certain conduct criminal without his thereby showing a wish and purpose to prevent that conduct. Prevention would accordingly seem to be the chief and only universal purpose of punishment. The law threatens certain pains if you do certain things, intending thereby to give you a new motive for not doing them. If you persist in doing them, it has to inflict the pains in order that its threats may continue to be believed.[10]

Holmes's view of the criminal law was clearly the antithesis of the theory of retribution, which, though already brought into question by

8. In Bentham's social philosophy, utilitarianism was joined with individualism and the idea of laissez-faire government (Dicey, *Relation between Law and Public Opinion*, 46). In this form, the utilitarian movement put special emphasis on the removal of improper government intervention: too much use of state power stifles the creative and productive pleasure-seeking inclinations of the individual (see Bentham, *Principles of Morals*, 3). For Bentham, a critic of the so-called anomalous stringencies of the English penal law, unnecessary restraint caused unnecessary pain and created disincentives for behavior that ought to have been encouraged. It followed that in his first tract on penal law Bentham started with a discussion of cases "unmeet" for punishment (Bentham, *Principles of Morals*, 170). He argued for reduction of sanctions in regard to various classes of crime because of the disutility of so harsh a sanction in achieving social benefit.

9. Though utilitarianism had a laissez-faire political significance for Benthamites in the England of that time, it was equally a science of how best the state could assert its power over individuals. It was a key force in establishing the idea that planned intervention in human behavior could be a tool of social control. In this sense, utilitarianism is at the bottom of jurisprudential as well as philosophical and social ideas that focus on the consequences that follow sentencing dispositions (see Dicey, *Relation between Law and Public Opinion*, 303ff.). Bentham's achievements have been described by another English scholar this way:

> Every department of our public life, our political institutions, every portion of our civil and criminal jurisprudence, every part of our legal procedure have been profoundly affected by his works. . . . Our improvements in the administration of justice, extending over a period of some fifty years, are to a very great extent direct applications of the principles enumerated and repeatedly expounded by him in his writings, which constituted a veritable treasure house of legal reforms, as well as a rich mine for statesmen and publicists (Coleman Phillipson, *Three Criminal Law Reformers: Beccaria, Bentham, Romilly* [London: J. M. Dent, 1923], 229).

10. O. W. Holmes, Jr., *The Common Law* (Boston: Little, Brown, 1881), 25.

utilitarianism, continued to occupy a major place in the theory of punishment. Francis Wharton, in his famous *Treatise on Criminal Law*,[11] offered an interpretation of criminal law that was thoroughly retributivist in orientation, paying homage to the moral idea of punishment found in Kant. Howe says, "The central purpose of Holmes' chapter on Criminal Law was to defend the preventive theory of punishment against such 'attacks' as those made by Wharton."[12] The emphasis on consequence is found even more prominently in the work of John Dewey. In writing about punishment, he criticized the purely vindictive motive for punishment:

> To content ourselves with pronouncing judgment of merit and demerit without reference to the fact that our judgments are themselves facts which have consequences, is complacently to dodge the moral issue. . . . The moral problem is that of modifying the factors which now influence future results. To change the working character or will of another we have to alter objective conditions which enter into his habits.[13]

And a leading American criminologist wrote,

> Not the crimes punished, but the crimes prevented should measure the worth of the law. . . . If out of a score of law-abiding persons, only one obeys the law from fear of its penalties, it does not follow that the penal system occupies a correspondingly insignificant place among the supports of social order. For the rules of the social game are respected by the good men chiefly because they are forced on the few bad.[14]

On another front, Kenny's *Outlines of Criminal Law*, widely used in American law schools and by practitioners, advanced the idea of general deterrence as the primary rationale for the criminal law.[15] And the following statement, by a judge sitting in a Pennsylvania trial court in 1930, considering appropriate sentence in a murder trial, is surely

11. Eleventh ed. (San Francisco: Bancroft-Whitney, 1912).
12. Mark DeWolfe Howe, *Justice Oliver Wendell Holmes: The Proving Years* (Cambridge: Harvard University Press, 1963), 170.
13. *Human Nature and Conduct* (New York: Modern Library, 1930), 17–19.
14. E. A. Ross, *Social Control* (New York, 1916), 125, as quoted in Edwin H. Sutherland, *Principles of Criminology* (Chicago: Lippincott, 1934).
15. Courtney Stanhope Kenny, *Outlines of Criminal Law*, 13th ed. (Cambridge: Cambridge University Press, 1929).

not unrepresentative of judicial thinking in America at the time: "the element of deterrence—the theory which regards the penalty as being not an end in itself but the means to obtaining an end, namely, the frightening of others who might be tempted to imitate the criminal . . . must fairly be regarded as one of the most important objectives of punishment."[16] It is even said that the idea of general deterrence is so strongly tied to the punishment rationale in America that there is an "official ideology of deterrence."[17]

Punishment as consequence, that is, punishment as a legal tool for shaping behavior, clearly became a fixture in American legal thinking, notwithstanding the development of a counter ideology that deterrence is an unrealistic goal of the criminal process.[18] The theme of

16. Commonwealth v. Ritter, Court of Oyer and Terminer, Philadelphia, 1930, 13 D. & C. 285, as cited in Sanford H. Kadish and Monrad G. Paulsen, *Criminal Law and Its Processes*, 3d ed. (Boston: Little, Brown, 1975), 1.

17. Franklin E. Zimring and Gordon J. Hawkins, *Deterrence: The Legal Threat in Crime Control* (Chicago: University of Chicago Press, 1973), 6–7.

18. Critics of general deterrence theory expressed doubts and downplayed any public expectations about the ability to control crime with punishment. Some thought that deterrence was simply a myth, that "crime was caused by criminal minds" and that deterrent punishments were ineffective with such persons. In his report for the Commission for the Study of Incarceration, Von Hirsch wrote in 1976, "This idea of general deterrence had prominence in the criminological literature of a century and a half ago: notably, in the writings of Jeremy Bentham. By the end of the nineteenth century, however, the idea had come into disfavor: as criminologists began attributing crime to offenders' background or biological makeup, they became convinced that criminal behavior could not be influenced by the threat of penalties" (Andrew von Hirsch, *Doing Justice: The Choice of Punishments* [New York: Hill and Wang, 1976], 37). This may be an overstatement, seeing that general deterrence remained a principal consideration in the American criminal process. Nevertheless, it is true that disillusionment with general deterrence became a central theme in academic literature and among public officials from the turn of the century onward. Roscoe Pound, in voluminous writings on criminal justice, indicated that he had only modest expectations for the deterrent effect of punishment on criminals, in spite of his markedly utilitarian view of the law. "Preventative justice," he wrote, "in any country governed by common-law constitutional notions, must be confined within very narrow limits. . . . [F]ear can never be a complete deterrent. The venturesome will always believe they can escape. The fearless will always be indifferent whether they escape. The crafty will always believe they can evade, and enough will succeed to encourage others" (Roscoe Pound, "Inherent and Acquired Difficulties in the Administration of Punitive Justice," in *Roscoe Pound and Criminal Justice*, ed. Sheldon Glueck [Dobbs Ferry, N.Y.: Oceana Publications, 1965], 101, 107). And writing what was to become a principal textbook in the field, Sutherland presented a devastating critique of deterrence. Punishment, he said, isolates the individual who is punished and makes him a confirmed enemy of society, teaches criminals how better to obtain immunity from the law, produces negative attitudes to authority, gives high status

deterrence, of general prevention, is quite thoroughly institutionalized in late twentieth-century America. Although scientific evidence on the workings of general deterrence is scanty, most legislators, criminal justice officials, and citizens undoubtedly believe in something like the mechanisms of deterrence. When harsher criminal penalties are called for, it is almost always in the belief that potential criminals, acting rationally, will be deterred from committing crimes by the threat of heavier penalties. Judges are not immune to these influences, and it is not surprising that general deterrence is often an important goal for them in their sentencing.

But it is not just general deterrence theory that the utilitarian movement brought. In the development of American thinking on punishment, there came to be two parallel strains of deterrence thought: one focused on the consequences that punishment can have on potential offenders, the other on its consequences for individual offenders. The latter is of course the justification for sentencing as a form of incapacitation, as well as a sanction that is supposed to deter the *individual*, who will not want to return to the unpleasant environment of a prison. Both notions of deterrence are based on the assumption that state power can be used to achieve consequences beneficial to the general social order, and in this sense general and individual deterrence, and rehabilitation, are based on the fundamental assumption of utilitarianism.

The notion of consequence for individual offenders is less clearly embedded in a cohesive body of thought that is part of our legal culture, but concern for the individual offender nonetheless remains part of our cultural heritage.[19] Beginning with Quaker notions of pen-

to offenders, and has the effect of discharging society from a felt obligation to pursue "constructive" crime prevention programs. Such criticisms were directed at what Sutherland called the classical school—including primarily the then old reform programs that were inspired by Bentham (Edwin H. Sutherland, *Principles of Criminology* [Chicago: Lippincott, 1934], 337).

19. In his classic work *Criminal Justice in America* Pound put hope in treating the individual offenders. Rather than deterrent punishment aimed at reducing the general likelihood of criminal conduct by others who might commit the same offence, wrote Pound, "the whole trend of psychology and penology indicates individualization, making the penal treatment fit the offender, dealing with the dangerous man rather than the dangerous act, as the line of progress" (Roscoe Pound, *Criminal Justice in America* [New York: Holt, 1930], 214). And Sutherland claimed to summarize the growing accepted wisdom of scholars and penal reformers when he described what should have been the substitute of punishment: "The policy that, from the factual point of view, is taking the place of punishment and

itence and expiation, the penitentiary system was deemed to have beneficial consequences for those committed to it. And rehabilitation through work and vocational training was one of the familiar doctrines of the early and mid-twentieth century.[20] Although belief in the rehabilitative potential of correctional institutions (so called in the belief that they can correct) has fallen on hard times, it is also part of our culture to attend to the consequences of official actions not only for those most immediately affected (in this case, defendants up for sentencing) but for those who will be indirectly affected by what we do to someone else. Adults who have learned to worry about the effects of their decisions on others are likely to extend that mode of "consequence" thinking to those who will be affected by their official decisions. That is precisely the position of the judges in our study.

Our interviews of judges concerning cases of white-collar crime revealed virtually no concern with individual rehabilitation of the offender. Instead these judges showed that their concern for punishment is often based on ideas about the general social control themes of utilitarianism of the eighteenth century.[21] Harm and blameworthiness

that from the ethical point of view, is presented as preferable to punishment, is the policy of studying the personality of the offender and the whole situation in which he becomes a criminal and controlling by means of the knowledge thus secured. This is the procedure of science . . . [it] is based on the conviction that the individual can be developed in practically any direction desired by the group and can acquire any attitude" (Sutherland, *Principles of Criminology*, 339–40). This, of course, is the theory of what came to be so well known as "individualization and rehabilitation." It shares with the theory of general deterrence the common ground of consequence orientation but denies either the utility of prison as a method for inducing conformity to social norms or as a tool that can affect more than the behavior of the incarcerated individual.

20. For a description and assessment of the rise of the rehabilitative ideal in American penology, see David J. Rothman, *The Discovery of the Asylum* (Boston: Little, Brown, 1971). Rothman marked the rise of the rehabilitative ideal at the beginning of the nineteenth century, particularly in the 1820s in New York and Pennsylvania. Penal reformers in the United States "believed that a setting which removed the offender from all temptations and substituted a steady and regular regimen would reform him. Since the convict was not inherently depraved, but the victim of an upbringing that had failed to provide protection against vices at loose in society, a well-ordered institution could successfully reeducate and rehabilitate him" (82).

21. The idea of deterrence continues to hold great attraction for the academy and for policymakers. See, for instance, Johannes Andenaes, "The Morality of Deterrence," 37 *U. Chi. L. Rev.* 649 (1970), and National Research Council, *Deterrence and Incapacitation: Estimating the Effects of Criminal Sanctions on Crime Rates* (Washington, D.C.: National Academy Press, 1978). The latter reports that "evidence certainly favors a proposition supporting deterrence more than it

are considered by these judges as prerequisites to the meting out of punishment, as moral-legal restrictions on the use of the criminal sanction. Subsequently, judges' primary focus is on the need to attain a general deterrent effect. Here harm and blameworthiness may be relevant, not as moral prerequisites to the use of criminal sanctions, but as measures of the strength of the need to deter other potential offenders. In this sense, the general social control themes of eighteenth-century utilitarianism give added meaning to harm and blameworthiness.

In addition, and despite their neglect of rehabilitation, the judges do consider the immediate effect of their sentence on the offender and those caught up in the offender's life. These considerations often constrain the judges from giving full reign to the deterrence rationale.

General Deterrence in the Judges' Thinking

Most of the judges we interviewed said that general deterrence was one of their purposes in sentencing white-collar cases, and many of those who thought it was one of their purposes thought it was the major or even the sole purpose, at least in some cases. Although they differed in the precise meaning of the concept, the core seemed to lie in the use of publicity and punishment to generate fear that would discourage other persons from committing offenses like those for which the defendant was being sentenced.

The judges give voice to this sentiment in a variety of ways. Here are a few examples:

My primary concern in a typical white-collar case is general deterrence—getting a message out to people in the business community who might be tempted to do the same thing.

I mentioned deterrence a moment ago, and I know that the theory of deterrence has received a lot of criticism. I don't agree with that criticism. I think that there is a message that emanates from a sentence. Now I don't know literally who that message goes to. Sentences receive a certain amount of publicity. There will be little

favors one asserting that deterrence is absent. The major challenge for future research is to estimate the magnitude of the effects of different sanctions on various crime types" (7).

things in the *Daily News*, the *New York Times*, rarely anything on television but quite often things on the radio, so word about the sentence does get out. Then beyond that the neighbors and associates and business associates of the person will hear about it. So there is a message that gets out. There is also the question of what would be the message if we gave a different sentence. . . . Now it is speculative to say exactly who it goes to, what is the psychological effect on the people who receive the message or hear it, how accurate their information is as to what goes on in these sentences, on and on. But it is something more than nothing, and that something has an importance, and we've got to worry about it. You can't just act as if you were sitting in an insulated soundproof chamber where nothing leaks out.

[Discussing a major fraud in the housing market under FHA regulations]: "The magnitude of his operation is such that it was a serious set of serious crimes. There is a need to let the community know that he was, that that system, however cleverly planned or executed, doesn't pay.

[Discussing a medicaid fraud case]: I hoped that some of this would rub off on others who might worry about it. The notion which is all too prevalent today that everybody has sort of a constitutional right to cheat the government bothers me. So I hoped that I would deter others who might be tempted.

Well, I think a number of white-collar crime people once caught are going to behave themselves, and so the deterrence of the individual isn't all that important. Rehabilitation? [It] does not appear to be that significant. Deterrence to others I think is a major consideration. Making certain that we do not unduly diminish the importance of the offense that has been committed against society is another consideration.

Sometimes the judges speak specifically to the nature of white-collar offenses or to white-collar persons.

I think there is a strong feeling, and I share it, that white-collar crime, if any kind of crime is deterrable, it ought to be among the most deterrable kinds of crime. The guy who sits down and makes out his income tax, he is engaging in a rather deliberate, purposive, thoughtful act, and he is appraising the consequences, unlike the guy who suddenly hauls off and shoots his spouse or something like that. And the prospect of punishment for wrongdoing ought to be, as we imagine this thing, more visible to this person's imagination and more meaningful, and therefore more potent. And therefore since general deterrence is probably the biggest single story we tell ourselves in sentencing, and I tell it to myself, is the tendency you believe that you ought to threaten these people with the thing that gets home to them best—imprisonment. And you ought to carry out the threat.

_____

[Notes from an untaped interview]: He admitted that in white-collar cases there was a potential for a unique deterrent. When asked why, he said, "Well, it is clear that in white-collar cases people have more to lose. More to lose in the way of reputation, more to lose in the way of money, more to lose in the way of family ties.

Jail as a Special Deterrent

A specific theme that arises often is the deterrent threat that lies in a possible jail sentence. Consider the following exchange:

JUDGE: I think deterrence is more predominantly in view with the white-collar sentence.

INTERVIEWER: Why?

JUDGE: Well, I guess because I think that is a class of people who are deterred by reading about people going to jail, more so than street crimes.

INTERVIEWER: So you think that there is an audience in white-collar cases that there really isn't in non-white-collar cases?

JUDGE: I wouldn't say isn't. I think the jail system generally has some deterrent effect. But I think it has a special impact. I think a lot of people decide to pay their taxes so they won't go to jail. I may be wrong, and that is why I wish someone would tell us because if I am wrong, then I would like to rethink my sentences.

_____

[Notes from an untaped interview]: He said he had been a defense lawyer—when he had been a defense lawyer he had dealt with many price-fixing cases in which he said the defendants "laughed" when they were indicted. . . . He said he didn't know whether this was still the case, but he believed that the only way to ensure a deterrent impact was to send white-collar criminals to jail.

A white-collar criminal has more of a fear of going to jail than this syndrome we find in the street crime. And I am not saying that if you cut everyone they don't bleed red blood. A person who commits a robbery or an assault, they don't want to go to jail either. But the white-collar criminal has more to lose by going to jail, reputation in the community, business as well as social community, decent living conditions, just the whole business of being put in a prison with a number on his back demeans this tremendous ego that is always involved in people who are high achievers. In that sense the deterrent effect is much stronger. In other words, if I say, or if the business community would perceive, well if you want to do this kind of thing that Mr. ____ did, you better not come before Judge ___ because you are going to jail if the facts are sufficiently grave. In that sense someone who might want to do it would be deterred. And also a white-collar criminal has much more of an opportunity to know of the end result and to deliberate and premeditate and make a choice rather than the street crime which as I said before is a reactive kind of crime.

The Role of Publicity

Judges believe that sentences of white-collar offenders are especially likely to be publicized in both the general media and occasionally in specialized, occupationally specific media. This publicity is both a minimum prerequisite for deterrence and an important source of pressure on judges to incarcerate white-collar offenders. As one judge put it,

The more public awareness, the more public knowledge, the more media coverage a case receives the more I'm likely to feel that a prison sentence is going to have a deterrent effect on others. I suppose this makes it more likely [for a white-collar offender] to get a prison sentence for the same act than a person who is not in the public eye.

Another judge, in talking about his sentencing of a nationally prominent official, highlighted the linkage of deterrence and publicity:

INTERVIEWER: I take it that the case received a lot of public attention. To the best of your recollection or ability to judge your own thinking at the time, when you sentenced him the first time, what role, what part did that public attention play?

JUDGE: Played a large part.

INTERVIEWER: Can you tell me a little bit more about that?

JUDGE: By public attention, the deterrent effect that would result from the public attention, not because—I wasn't affected in the slightest about how the public might feel about it. That didn't enter into it. But the fact that it had received wide publicity would add to the deterrent effect.

Still another judge, talking about a case of fraud involving the FHA, noted the special importance of publicity within the relevant occupational community:

As a practical matter deterrence is effective only if that which is done is known by those who need deterrence, and that in a sense defines publicity. Now whether you mean by that publicity through the news media as such, it happened that it was in the news media, but it is the kind of thing in which the industry, the lending agencies, the contracting organizations, follow and are very much aware of what is going on in cases of this kind. The dissemination of the word occurs much more broadly and at least more effectively in a case of that kind through that media than it does through the press media.

Given the right circumstances judges may be able to take steps to insure that their sentences receive publicity sufficient to provide the possibility of a deterrent effect.

INTERVIEWER: Do you have a sense that when you sentence a tax offender like the one that you sentenced that your sentence will get publicity, it will be known, that there is an audience for it?

JUDGE: Yes, I do, and in fact I try to make sure of it. With the tax cases typically in this state, it's a small area, tax cases are not everyday occurrences, and so there is almost always a newspaper article that a tax offender was put in jail. Sometimes rather prominent, sometimes not so prominent a place in the paper, but it is there, and I do think—now, where I can do something about it I do. For example, when I had a rash of postal embezzlers . . . I said to the government one time, look I am giving him thirty days for deterrent purposes and I want to know what you are doing to have these sentences known within the postal service, because if they are not known, then I am going to reconsider whether I do it, at least for deterrent purposes. And they went and brought it to the attention of whoever it is, the postal inspector, and they worked out a system to be sure all sentences were made known to the postmaster in these towns—they post it or put out a newsletter or whatever they do—I did the same thing with the banks. I asked the banking association what they were going to do about publicizing the fact that a teller went to jail. I tried to not only think it gets known but to do what I could to make it known.

The Importance of Specific Target Audiences

We generally think of specific deterrence as applying directly to the offender in question and of general deterrence as applying to the whole community. But as some of the above quotes suggest, an impressive feature of the judges' thoughts about deterrence is their desire to cause deterrent effects in specific target audiences. Sometimes, to be sure, the target audience may be fairly broad and loosely defined, as general references to "the business community" suggest. In other instances it is a specific target but one that covers a vast portion of the population. Consider the following two comments on income tax violations:

> Income tax case is the one that is most particularly troublesome as far as white-collar crime is concerned... because every mild sentence that is afforded in an income tax case is an inducement to those who ought to be deterred to go and do likewise.
>
> ———————————
>
> Getting down specifically to the matter of deterrence, one very experienced judge, Judge _____ _____ of the District Court of _____ in a seminar that I attended right after I was appointed, talked about this very subject. He always made the policy of sentencing income tax evaders to some minimal term, three to six months. He told how he had given a doctor I think a five-month sentence and a few weeks after that learned from the district director of the Internal Revenue... that within thirty days he received other tax returns from doctors in that area. Well that is an example of what I mean by deterrence.

Apparently it is believed to work in cases of tax protestors as well as tax evaders:

We had a rather large number of the tax protestors cases in the district of Arizona committed mostly by Mormons who live in this area. They have a religious belief that has led them in some instances to not pay taxes on the basis of their belief that there is something immoral about it. There have even been Mormons who have written books about how to avoid paying taxes, and the authors themselves have been tax evaders. For a while we were treating these people leniently while scolding them in court for their disregard of their obligation to the state. But this scolding did not seem to work so we then started meting out some prison terms. One can see from what happened in this area the deterrent effect of the prison sentence, for very soon after we starting meting out the prison sentence the tax protestors no longer appeared in our court. It seems that this problem may have been cleared up now.

In cases in which the crime is more specialized, the audience will be similarly specialized. Although deterrence may apply to the entire community, judges believe that in white-collar cases there are more limited and focused audiences for their sentences. Generally such limited audiences are comprised of people in the same business, occupation, or profession as the defendant, people whose day-to-day activities are similar to those that gave rise to the offense for which a sentence is to be imposed. Here are examples of the judges' comments on a variety of occupational worlds:

Savings and loans association employees:

Well, we eventually indicted and prosecuted all the officers of his bank. It was a savings and loan association. I'm sure what was going on here was going on in many savings and loan associations. They were all convicted. And I am sure that the fact of that conviction made a tremendous deterrent effect on everybody else in the savings and loan association who had done this. It got wide publicity in that area.

Public officials (in this case a senator who had accepted a bribe):

JUDGE: I think if you send enough senators and congressmen to jail for accepting bribes they will quit it.

INTERVIEWER: So your sense was that there was an audience for this sentence?

JUDGE: No question about it. A tremendous audience. One hundred senators—and some congressmen.

Bank employees:

JUDGE: Another consideration very important to me is a sentence that would act as a deterrent, a deterrent to this man for ever considering doing something like that again. If for chance he got into a position of trust some way. And a deterrent to others knowing what the punishment was, a deterrent to them if they might be considering conduct like that.

INTERVIEWER: So that you have in the back of your mind other persons in similar positions who might be tempted to do this kind of thing, is that what you were saying, as a general deterrent effect?

JUDGE: Well, I think, let's say that you got one hundred thousand bank employees around the country. For them to know that the top of one of the biggest banks got three years for embezzling from the bank—I think that is a deterrent to people in white-collar jobs in the banking industry, or white-collar jobs with big companies in the financial areas.

Veterinarians:

INTERVIEWER: In this particular case, what was it in the criminal event with the activities of the individual that led you to feel that in terms of the tax spectrum, he was more on the serious side?

JUDGE: It was a first as far as veterinarians are concerned.

INTERVIEWER: A first as far as veterinarians are concerned?

JUDGE: Yes, veterinarians. Probably they've been getting by with it quite profusely, and I don't doubt that his case taught a lesson to veterinarians. So that is a special case where he had to suffer a little more than had there been many veterinarians over the years doing the same thing in order to warn others not to start it or to get rid of their double records. And the veterinarian science is closely related to medical science, and doctors, people, have a tendency to occasionally collect their fees without reporting them, and to maintain offices at two or three different clinics, two or three different places, double set of books. So that the very fact that he was—the fact that the case was receiving some publicity—caused me to feel that there was a substantial deterrent effect, would be that in the nature of the sentence. The ordinary cases, narcotics, for example, don't receive that much publicity and those who commit the crimes aren't that much aware what is going on in the field anyway. You don't read the press, listen to it, pay much attention to it. Those blue-collar crimes, it's the same way. When you get into that area there is, I think, a substantial deterrent, public deterrent, in the sentence.

INTERVIEWER: What area?

JUDGE: White-collar crimes. . . . We think in terms of the white-collar crime as being the crime committed in the course of the performance of a professional duty or an occupational performance by persons who are collegians or public officials or those who commonly wear white collars.

INTERVIEWER: Then you say in that kind—

JUDGE: Suits, ties—

INTERVIEWER: And in that kind of case you think the sentence has a heavier impact?

JUDGE: Generally, I think so, yes.

INTERVIEWER: On the defendant or—

JUDGE: On the public. In deterring others from doing it. So you are aware of, or at least concerned that, in that type of case the public has knowledge of what is going on and that . . .

INTERVIEWER: In the veterinarian case, you had the sense that the public knew this case was—

JUDGE: The veterinarians knew that it was going on. Indeed, veterinarians attended the trial.

INTERVIEWER: Oh, really?

JUDGE: Yes, there were a number in the audience.

Stockbrokers:

INTERVIEWER: The other defendants, particularly the executives, can you pick one of them perhaps—one that received the higher sentence among the three executives, you mentioned eighteen months—what was his role?"

JUDGE: Well that particular individual was a managing partner in a very small brokerage house. But the machinery, the facilities of his brokerage house, were essential to move this paper along, to move the bad paper out in this direction and then have the money from the victims come back. And his account was used to deposit the money and then distribute it. His offices were used for the meeting places. His whole brokerage facilities lay right at the center of this sort of thing—the engine [without] which the car would not run—and my feeling was, and also he participated quite handsomely in the proceeds of the scheme, and my feeling was that he was a very important participant, and that also he was in a position to appreciate the very real degree to which this kind of market business depends on trust, on the genuineness of documents, or the trust you can have in people's words.

INTERVIEWER: These were—the certificates were being sold through his office?

JUDGE: Yes, they were counterfeit securities, and he knew it. And they were being sold through his office.

INTERVIEWER: And the brokers in his office were selling them to the clients—is that what—

JUDGE: Well, he would sell them to other brokerage houses who would then sell them to clients. There was no one else in his office involved in it, and he had a very small shop indeed. And the details of it escape me but I can tell you that his brokerage house facilities lay at the center of and were essential to the machinery of getting the bad paper out on the street and turning it into money. And I think in this case I felt the need to deter others. I remember saying at the sentencing that so much depends on pieces of paper these days. Millions of dollars change hands on the basis of little pieces of paper. And the whole system comes crashing down unless the little pieces of paper are genuine, and their integrity is not perverted by people in a position to do so. And I think that in that particular situation having in mind his position, I felt a need to impose a social deterrent because it has been absolutely amazing to me in some of these cases the ease with which the paper trail can be fooled around with. Eventually at least, and then eventually they will catch you, but for a while you can just make off like a thief in the night by fooling around with and perverting the integrity of the pieces of paper.

INTERVIEWER: When that occurs, when you see that, does that— is that a mark for you of a type of criminal activity which deserves particularly harsh sentencing because of that quality?

JUDGE: It is not so much particularly harsh sanctioning as it is a fact to which I consider in that threshold white-collar determination I spoke of earlier, namely, prison or no prison. The white-collar criminal that I see quite usually has no prior criminal record at all, and he is a decent, well-educated, well-spoken fellow. He generally has a family which can and does write you heartrending letters, he has got all kinds of people who will write letters about what a fine person he is, of the church, or he does pro bono things, one thing or another. And in a lot of these cases, a powerful argument can be made that this man should not go to prison—he has never done anything before, and nobody got hurt and so forth. I tend to resist that, to the extent that I do resist it, primarily perhaps, or at least significantly, because I think it is important for the integrity of the commercial system to be preserved. And I think there is something to be said for the deterrent effect upon other people in business in brokerage houses who are in a position to engage in this kind of activity if they read about a publicized term of imprisonment passed upon someone with this social profile.

People who make illegal campaign contributions (from an untaped interview):

He said that in the ____case the jail sentence had less to do with ____and more to do with his fear that unless there was some substantial jail time that violations of the corrupt practices act would go on. He said that this case had received nationwide publicity and so he believed that it was an appropriate vehicle to put union leaders and businessmen on notice. That the practice of making illegal contributions either from pension funds or from corporate assets had to be stopped.

Internal Revenue Service agents:

At one time they were conducting a drive—there was a lot of corruption in the IRS and they were after the agents and the people who were using the agents. Those cases, most of them we sent to jail. The purpose was very obvious. Word got around and the results of these cases were on the bulletin boards in the IRS offices all around the country, and it had its effect... It scared the other people from following in those steps.

Chiropractors:

> INTERVIEWER: Now when you sentenced these chiropractors, I could—what was your purpose, let me ask the question that way, that will give me a better understanding of—
>
> JUDGE: My purpose was (1) to punish the individual, and (2) to deter other people from engaging in or continuing this kind of scheme.
>
> INTERVIEWER: Did you have a sense that it would be—that the deterrent effect on others, that the message would get there?"
>
> JUDGE: It was well publicized.
>
> INTERVIEWER: Were you aware at the time of sentencing that it was being publicized?
>
> JUDGE: I was aware of it, sure. As a matter of fact I think at the time of sentencing the defendant's attorneys came in and asked for actual surrender to be delayed for two weeks so that they could appear before a Senate committee that was investigating it, which I granted, because I did want it publicized.

Thus do judges give voice, in concrete and specific ways, to the effort to deter particular types of wrongdoers who are in familiar occupational categories. For these judges, "general prevention" is not an abstract notion, but one that is given detailed meaning through efforts to deter persons in particular occupations from the forms of white-collar crime that are most common in that line of work.[22]

How Judges Think about Effects on Offenders and Those around Them

The Process Is the Punishment

The first of the personal effects that many judges take into account is the effect of the process of investigation, indictment, and conviction on the offender. Most judges believe that the suffering experienced by a white-collar person as a result of apprehension, public indictment,

---

22. On occasion, these concerns are reflected in the court record. We are grateful to Professor Frank Allen for calling our attention to the actions of Judge Avril Cohn of the eastern district of Michigan. Judge Cohn, in dealing with Arab-Americans who had violated the federal law relating to the shipment of firearms to the Middle East, conditioned a reduction of sentence on the defendants' placing an account of their actions and the consequences in a foreign language newspaper and radio station. These notices are part of the public record of the court.

and conviction as well as the collateral disabilities incident to each—loss of job, revocation of professional license, diminishment of status in the community—is itself a kind of punishment. They wonder whether the imposition of additional suffering is justifiable and warranted. As one judge put it;

> There is no doubt about the fact that in most white-collar crimes as such the return of the indictment is much more traumatic than even the sentence. Pronouncing of the sentence is not as injurious to the person, his relationship to the community, to his family, as the return of the indictment. The return of the indictment in many instances causes a tremendous loss, is felt, the loss of business relationships, often the loss of jobs, of bank credit, a loss of friends, social status, occasionally loss of a wife, members of the family, children around the father, more when they hear that an indictment has been returned and he has been charged than they do after they have gotten used to the idea and he is sentenced for it. There is no question about the fact that that is much more severe on the white-collar criminal than it is on the blue-collar defendant.

Another judge explained at some length the differential impact of the criminal process on white-collar and street criminals.

> First, the white-collar criminal by virtue of his conviction has suffered a loss of position, usually loss of employment, sometimes status in his profession, other times the ability to ever find employment in anything requiring a fidelity bond or what have you. Whereas the common street criminal hasn't had a career loss of a similar nature; indeed in some areas the conviction of a crime is some sort of a badge of maturity. Whereas, in a white-collar neighborhood, conviction for crime is generally going to cause economic hardship and a lot of social loss of prestige, and I think that is something you have to give weight to. If you take a man who has been a pillar of his community and has a good family, and no criminal background and he's convicted of embezzling from a bank, he loses his job, he loses his home, and he probably loses his family, it often occurs and he also loses his future prospect of employment—he has already been punished fairly substantially. The ordinary street criminal hasn't suffered that kind of loss, there isn't that sort of thing that could be put on the scales. That is one distinction in

white-collar sentencing. A lot of people might see more in others and might have argued that that is not a proper consideration and that they don't agree with it, but I don't agree with them, I think it is a consideration.

There is, of course, an entire, complex social theory built into that assessment of the differential impact of the criminal process on white-collar and street criminals. It is as if low social status is already a kind of personal humiliation to which the criminal process adds little. It is as if the social and family ties of the street criminal mean less both to him and to the society. For the white-collar criminal, in contrast, high status means respect and a valued position, both of which may be lost because of the process itself. Indeed, some of the judges seemed to pay particular attention to the loss of respectability that accompanies indictment and prosecution of the white-collar offender. As one judge explained his sentence of a respected businessman in an income tax case, he suggested that by the time the defendant came up for sentencing, he "had suffered enough. The ignominy, the shame, the humiliation. . . . was awesome. You put a man like that in jail for three years—you could, but why?"

As two other judges put it in discussing nonincarcerative sentences in two similar cases:

> Well, you have a person who has . . . a certain status—has surrounded him with certain aura, and you strip that aura away and let him stand naked and in front of his peers, that itself is pretty serious punishment.
>
> ---
>
> JUDGE: The theory is that he has been punished enough, this poor man has been so punished and so forth—
> INTERVIEWER: Because he has been indicted?
> JUDGE: Because he has been indicted—the shame. The disgrace, he has lost face with peers and so forth, which with people involved in street crime is probably not as great. I think that has some merit.

Other judges are more concerned with the impact of the criminal process on the offender's occupation, profession, or subsequent ability to earn a living. As one judge said about his sentence in a case involving securities fraud,

So I would think that it is fair to say that the fact the man is going to lose his opportunity to engage in a profession or a particular business that he is engaged... would certainly be a mitigating consideration.

INTERVIEWER: In regard to the professionals in general some have said that the prosecution itself, the revelation of the fact that the person is a target or a subject of a federal indictment leads to a professional downfall, and shame and the person probably can't keep his job or lose his status in the community, his whole livelihood may be undermined. Is that something which you feel you need to take into account?

JUDGE: I took that into account with reference to the man I mentioned a few moments ago, who I fined. He had lost his job and he had gotten a new job. And he lost that when his employer learned about it. That was a factor, definitely, with reference to the lawyer who I gave a month to. It was a very difficult decision to make because he had resigned his partnership at his law firm and I don't know what he faces in the way of any other further punishment in the hands of the grievance committee or the appellate division of our state supreme court. But I took that into account, yes I did, definitely.

Another judge emphasized the loss of a professional license incident to conviction in discussing the way he dealt with lawyers involved in two different fraud cases:

INTERVIEWER: You mentioned also in this case the fact that the lawyer would be disbarred would also constitute a substantial—

JUDGE: Don't you agree? In a man who has gone through 3 years of law school, and then gone through a bar review course and taken the bar examination, and has a nice practice, and is making—I think in this case—something like forty thousand dollars a year and suddenly he is disbarred, I would consider that a stiffer punishment than anything I would be likely to impose. I just have gotten through a trial of two young attorneys for perpetrating a fraud, or rather for participating in an attempt to return stolen bonds to the Manufacturers Hanover Trust Company. And those fellows, unless the conviction is reversed, are going to be automatically disbarred, and they are two young fellows in their late twenties or early thirties, just getting started. And their career is shot. And I don't know what in the world I will do by way of sentencing those fellows, but certainly the law which provides for automatic disbarment is a stiffer sentence than any I could think of imposing.

INTERVIEWER: Looking across the board at white-collar defendants in general, it is probably true that whether the person is a high-ranking officer of a corporation or a company or a professional, doctor or lawyer, the stiffest punishment is likely to be the loss of that position, income and status and prestige in the community, so that given the prior status of these individuals there may be a necessary lowering of the prison sentence as punishment because they are already getting another punishment that others don't receive.

JUDGE: I think you are right. That is why in many cases the white-collar sentences seem lower, but when you consider the overall effect on the man's life of the conviction, they haven't gotten away lightly at all.

There is another aspect of the criminal process in white-collar cases that judges take into account as they consider the effects of their sentences. Because of the complexity and ambiguity of white-collar offenses the period of investigation can itself be quite extended. In that case, some judges believe the anxiety and uncertainty that result from a long period of living under suspicion are themselves a form of pre-sentence punishment. Talking about a political corruption case, one judge suggested that by the time the offender came up for sentencing

> six or seven years had passed. He had been under the strain of this case all of that time. It had broken up his family. It had affected him very adversely, his whole life. . . . Well I, by that time, felt that he had suffered enough, having gone through six or seven years of this business, at a cost to him of tens maybe hundreds of thousands of dollars, although the cost was a minimum part of it. I put him on probation then.

INTERVIEWER: Do you find that your sentencing decision, especially in white-collar crime cases, is affected at all by your sense of—to use the vernacular—what the man has been through before he arrives in front of you?

JUDGE: A little bit, yes. Particularly the tax case because unlike other cases it lasts so long for the individual. A lot of people don't have as full a perception of that, also some judges I don't think do, as prosecutors who have lived with the tax case and have a full sense or have defended and know what it is to go with the guy for regional counsel, to go to Washington, to go to the tax division. From the time the IRS guy first comes and says, this is a criminal investigation, until the time he stands before the judge wondering what the sentence is going to be, that is at least a two-year period and sometimes three. That is a long time to be under the anxiety of whether you are going to jail. Most other cases, like the teller embezzler, they find the shortage in March and they indict in April, and I get it in June. So there is a clear difference. The tax case happens to be a long, drawn out period of anxiety for the individual, which I think does impact him and his family in worse ways than some other criminal offenses. What I do with that, it is harder to know. I am aware of it, maybe I am somewhat sympathetic to it. Maybe it is one reason I am willing to give thirty- and sixty-day sentences that otherwise might be a year or two.

Finally, the prospect of ruining a life in the course of administering a criminal punishment is all the more real in the eyes of the judge when imprisonment is used in white-collar cases. The special sensitivity of white-collar offenders to jail that judges cite as a reason for believing in the deterrability of white-collar crime is, at the same time, a factor weighing against its imposition. As one judge put it,

The average white-collar defendant if not utterly destroyed is powerfully injured by all the attendant hurts that accompany being put into prison. He is put out of business, he is thrown out of his profession, he losses his job, he loses his status, and so on. I think those things are part of the impact of the sanction on that person that somehow has to be put in the scale.

The consensus among judges is that the suffering inflicted by the criminal process is an important factor in the sentencing calculation;

a few judges, however, are unconvinced by "the process is the punishment" argument. Some discount it out of a desire to insure equity in their treatment of white-collar and street criminals.

> I had one sentence within the past year or year and a half where a man was at the top of his banking profession and his embezzlements and defalcations and all of his manipulations resulted in some other banks going under and so forth, and the argument was made to me in sentencing that he had been punished enough, he lost his job, he has been disgraced and so forth, and you shouldn't add to that and my reaction to that was a teller who decided to steal two thousand dollars and is sitting in prison reading newspapers isn't very impressed when somebody who has stolen several million is given probation because he has already been punished enough by the disgrace. That doesn't fit very well with the teller in prison, nor should it.

INTERVIEWER: Are there other aspects of process, for example, the argument is made well this is white collar offenders, as indeed as you describe them as professionals and businessmen, in a position in the community, and their families, and the process itself, merely the fact of being indicted, for example—

JUDGE: The fall from grace—

INTERVIEWER: That's right, has such an impact on—

JUDGE: No, I am not as impressed with that as some others are. It seems to me that the fall from grace shouldn't really count in his favor. It is simply a function of how well off he was before the trial. And the truck driver, who didn't fall from grace, I can't see treating him the worse just because he didn't know where to fall from. This guy fell from grace, yes, but all that means is that for twenty years he was esteemed in his community, was a member of the country club, he had all the comforts of life. So, I am not terribly impressed with the idea that I should be lenient on him because already all his friends at the country club are scorning him, even assuming that is so—and I'm not so sure that's so, but even if it were so I don't think I put much stock in that.

Other judges fall back on their experiences as lawyers defending white-collar criminals and think about the "country club" reaction in another way.

[Notes from an untaped interview]: I asked him whether or not as a sentencing judge, he put much credence in the idea that white-collar offenders suffer so much in the prosecution of a crime that they deserve no further punishment. He responded by citing his experience as a defense attorney in which he said he often found that white-collar offenders gain prestige in the country clubs. They were able to claim that they were unfairly persecuted and they often derived certain status from such a claim. Too often, he said, he had seen white-collar offenders laughing and having a good time, to believe that the mere prosecution was punishment enough. He said that he thought it was a good defense lawyer's argument, but not one which as a former defense lawyer he could reasonably credit.

Age and Health as Personal Factors Affecting Sentence

The typical white-collar offender is considerably older than his common crime counterpart. As judges think about the effects of their sentences and try to insure that they are not disproportionately severe, age and health considerations sometimes loom large. As one judge said in explaining a one-year sentence in an embezzlement case,

> If he had been a younger man and in better health, the sentence could have been longer, which it could have gone to two, three or four years. The limiting factor which squeezed the sentence down was his age and health. They pushed me toward virtually giving him the shorter sentence that would have any impact or real meaning. I think, and I may have it confused with another case, it is possible that I gave him just one year and then being concerned over his health and the fact that he couldn't be paroled on one year, I then amended it to make a year and a day to make him eligible for parole.

Yet another example of the fact that age is taken into account is provided in the following discussion of a medicare fraud case:

> I had a doctor who engaged in medicare and medicaid fraud on quite a substantial scale. He filed reimbursement vouchers for patients he had never seen or whom he had seen once or twice and he claimed to have seen eight, ten, twelve times. He testified in his own behalf, which is relatively rare in a criminal case, and lied on the witness stand. He was in his early sixties. I sentenced him to,

I believe it was a year, it may have been eighteen months. It was his first offense. Because of his age, that weighed in my mind in favor of being lenient.

These accounts occur with some regularity in our material. Health and age are factors that are clearly attended to by judges, though many are on the lookout for false claims of medical problems as an excuse for sentence that does not include prison. But judges are human beings and they do not relish sending white-haired grandpas to prison, especially for the first time. And they all know of an illustrative case or two in which a heart attack followed a sentence of imprisonment.

Prevention of Injury to Innocent Parties

As they consider the effects of the various possible sentences they can impose, judges move beyond the offender to survey the impact on those who are dependent upon him. By not imposing a prison sentence, or by imposing only a short one, judges appear to want to avoid eliminating the contribution to community and family that white-collar offenders make in the normal course of their lives. A portion of an interview quoted earlier bears repeating in this context:

Almost always he is a husband and a father. Almost always he has children who are in the process of becoming what we like to think children ought to be—well brought up, well educated, nurtured, cared for—usually he is a member of the kinds of civic organizations in the community who value his services and derive value from his services. . . . As a result you are up against this more difficult problem in degree in the so-called white-collar criminals as to whether you are not going to inflict a hurt on society by putting such a person in a prison and making him cease to be a good father and a good husband and good worker in the community.

This perspective on sentencing white-collar offenders carries with it a distinct view of the relationship of the criminal act to the rest of the personality of the white-collar offender. The crime tends to be seen as a separable part of the offender's total personality; it is one negative characteristic in a cluster of other positive characteristics. Judges told us that what they most often learn from pre-sentence reports is that the offender has usually led a productive life. In a typical case the defendant is married and has children; he is reported to be a good parent, an employer with dependent employees or a professional person with clients dependent on him; he may be active in his church and a fund-raiser for local charities. "He just happened to cheat the IRS out of thirty thousand dollars in the last three years," as one judge said.

In looking at this prototypical white-collar offender, the judge may want to impose a deterrent sentence, but would like to do it without also punishing the defendant's spouse and children, who will lose their source of emotional and financial support, his employees or clients, who will lose their employment or professional services, and the general community, which will lose an otherwise exemplary citizen. Prevention of these potential losses to the defendant's network of dependents and associates is a significant consideration in judges' sentencing of white-collar offenders. In sharp distinction, the defendant convicted of bank robbery or a simple theft is typically perceived to be without family and work-related dependents. Since he is less anchored in a social matrix, less damage is done by sending him away:

> The other kind of difference that very often appears is that they are usually family people. The chances of them being family people who are supporting their wife and children are reasonably high. With the street criminal it is extremely rare to run into anybody who has a stable family situation and where you are going to inflict upon innocent other persons a substantial penalty by putting him in jail. It's fairly easy to put the unmarried man or woman or the man who's run out on his family and is just living it up in jail, because nobody is suffering but the defendant himself. Sometimes you see these family situations, I've had cases where the wife was dying of cancer, there were a couple of small kids at home, the husband was stealing to try and pay medical bills and what have you. When you go up against situations like that, it is apparent that if you put the breadwinner in jail the people who are going to suffer worse, are the innocent family members. That situation can occur in a non-white-collar crime. It's true theoretically, and I've seen cases where you have to ignore the suffering of others because you simply can't let the defendant benefit by virtue of his family situation. But on the other hand, it's not the consideration which I think any judge could turn his back completely on.

Another judge expressed the same view with the following statement:

> Whether there are people who are dependent on him or her, whether they are really making a contribution to the people, whether there is going to be an injury to others if I incarcerate him: that has a profound effect on me and when I sense that, I am more inclined to be lenient. In this particular case, the defendant . . . was pleading guilty to a calculated fraud, which you could tell from his own admissions and from what the indictment was, but you also had evidence of his prior background, you had the report on his family, and all that. My recollection is now, although I've sentenced so many people since then, but I think he was separated from his wife. I don't think there was a problem [in this case] where you are taking somebody out of the home and really inflicting the major punishment on innocent people.

The importance of the impact of a sentence on family members may be extended to employees and the larger community. In a major tax evasion prosecution in which the defendants were convicted of understating their corporate income by hiding ownership interest in a significant sector of their actual business, the judge gave the following explanation for a sentence that required the defendants to report to a local prison facility on weekends only:

> If you take these two income tax evaders, if you take them and say, "Okay, you are going to spend three years—I am going to throw the book at you—three years to the custody of the attorney general," forty people, forty of their employees are out of work. I don't know how many hundreds of kids in the ghetto who need jobs to rehabilitate themselves, how many of those will go back to crime because they are not working, you see. Fine, give them three years, forget all these other salutary purposes that a light sentence in this case— a work release, staying in their own business and working with a charitable foundation—accomplishes.

Another judge, sentencing a defendant convicted of operating fraudulent businesses in which unsophisticated persons were sold machines that would not perform their advertised functions, decided not to impose a prison sentence. He stated,

I felt a jail-type sentence was not called for because if I had sent the person away there would have been dozens of people who would have lost their jobs completely and would not have had any means of finding new employment. I made it a condition of probation that the defendant make all reasonable efforts to find jobs for persons who had been employed in his business, all of whom were going to lose their livelihood when the company would be liquidated. I therefore reserved the possibility of committing this guy if he didn't comply with this probation condition.

Other judges cited the need for maintaining an individual's professional contribution to his community as a reason for not imposing a prison sentence. In a conviction for medicaid fraud, a physician was given probation so that he could continue to practice medicine. The judge stated,

I didn't want to send him to jail because I felt that it would deprive him and his family of the livelihood he could make as a doctor and it would deprive the neighborhood of his services. So what I was trying to accomplish was to see that to some extent he could repay society. In this particular case there was a way he could do something of social usefulness. I felt that this was a strong enough reason to overcome whatever good would be done for society by imposing a sentence for general deterrence, which is the only justification that exists for [prison] sentences in these cases.

Our interviews disclosed a number of cases in which judges took into account the unique service that professional and business persons provide to a community. In some of these cases, judges considered the possibility of a nonprison disposition for the reasons cited above but rejected it because of overriding considerations concerning the seriousness of the particular white-collar crime. In particular, as described in chapter 3, there was a strong feeling among many judges that because business and professional persons are vested with public trust, their offenses require sanctions more severe than those meted out for violations that do not entail a breach of public trust. One judge described the interplay between these two factors this way:

So the way I resolved it, and of course why I would give him prison, is because of the trust issue that I talked about. I believe if someone can come in and commit a crime like that [investor fraud] and go out with nothing but probation people would just laugh off the idea that there is any punishment for those types of activity. And so I balance, I give what I think is a moderate sentence [an investment banker is not going to want to serve a year in jail]. To me it is enough, yet it isn't a lot, it doesn't keep him out of commission for years and years. He has responsibilities to a family and elderly people and all, and I didn't want to keep him out of commission for a long time. You know, you weigh these imponderables, the good things in his behalf, the need to get him back functioning. Yet he has committed a serious crime involving the trust other people have put in him, and there is the need to vindicate the law in a gentle way. And you come out with a year. There isn't any formula. You could come out differently.

Facilitating Compensation and Making Reparations

Another closely related concern of judges is the opportunity to use the sentencing purposefully and positively to benefit victims, if there are discrete victims, or the community as a whole if there are not. In certain instances the offender's ability to make restitution or to perform community service is important in mitigating punishment. In cases in which restitution is the concern, the defendant's potential earning power or financial status at the time of sentencing is closely examined. In either instance restitution was often considered to be a sentence that could replace imprisonment. In other cases, ability to make restitution was a factor that reduced a penalty by either affecting the length of a prison term or the manner in which a prison disposition was to be served (weekend or full-time).

If restitution is dependent on the offender's continual employment, a prison term would eliminate a potential contribution to the "community of victims," just as a prison term would eliminate the offender's contribution to family, business associates, and the public community. The following interaction illustrates the judges' views:

JUDGE: Now if restitution can be made, I think there are many cases where no incarceration is called for. Now here is a man whom I sentenced for a violation of securities laws. He pleaded guilty. And he had participated in defrauding investors for touting his particular stock. The amount that he made, as it turned out, was something less than the investors lost. He undertook to make full restitution to the investors so that they ended up not losing anything, even though that was more than he made out of the deal. And I suspended the imposition of sentence in this case and placed him on probation with a special condition that he make full restitution to the investors. That in effect punished him because he paid out more than he took in, it helped the investors, and it had the same deterrent effect a period of incarceration would have.

INTERVIEWER: Could you elaborate more on how restitution has a different impact?

JUDGE: Well, he ended up losing about double what he got out of it. He made about $25,000 and ended up paying back $50,000, as I recall. Those figures may not be quite correct, but that is about the ratio. So he ended up an awful lot out of pocket. And I couldn't have fined him that much but he agreed to work and to pay it back. The investors, believe me, were quite happy with the sentence. He was not terribly happy with it. But he preferred that to going to jail, and I think considering all of the various factors, that it was a better sentence all around.

Another judge gave similar reasons for deciding on a nonprison sentence for a person convicted of not reporting large amounts of income:

JUDGE: When it came to sentencing, he said, "Listen, I'll go and get that money from the Swiss bank, but it can't be gotten out except with me," and I knew that was true and the assistant U.S. attorney wasn't willing at all to do that. And he said, "Now make application for probation and take my gamble." Well, there was a lot of publicity about it. I decided to take a chance on him because I believed that he would be back for his child. He went there and withdrew half a million dollars and came back and turned it over to the government. And I proceeded to put him on probation even though he had served one term and he didn't plead guilty in this case either. He had had a trial and there was a jury that found him guilty. But still I said he had served one term, he needs to make a living, but he kept his word with us.

INTERVIEWER: Well, in this case, you must have considered sending him to a term in prison. What made you decide that that wasn't appropriate in this case?

JUDGE: Well, the restitution. There is half a million dollars back in the coffers that we wouldn't have got if I had sent him to prison. He would have served his term, and there would have been no way of getting it, and eventually some day or other he would have gotten out of the country somehow and gotten that money. That was it.

Imposition of a sentence that requires the defendant to make payments to the victims of his crime is closely allied to another type of sentence rooted in the idea of reparations. We found that several kinds of community service obligations are used in lieu of prison by a large number of our respondents and that such sentences are thought to be particularly suited to cases of white-collar crime. Through a community service sentence, the payment is made to the general community rather than to the specifically identifiable victim. The notion that the general community has been injured by the wrongs of the offender and that the community as a whole can be repaid is fundamental to the concept of reparation. While restitution and reparations are clearly distinct from deterrence and punishment, interviews with judges indicate that they use community service sentences as a way to impose a deterrent sanction while at the same time effecting repayment.

Our respondents told of sentences that required a dentist to provide free dental care, a physician to provide free examinations, an industrialist to set up a nonprofit corporation, a social welfare worker to go on part-time payment at his place of work while continuing to work full-time, and corporate executives to donate time to communal charitable organizations. The following excerpt is from a judge explaining two community service sentences, the first meted out to a partner in a large metropolitan law firm, the second to a dentist, both cases of tax evasion:

JUDGE: Well, I had two ideas in mind. One was I didn't really want to give him straight probation, I thought that was getting away too easily. To consider the taxes involved, it wasn't an enormous sum, but it was a substantial amount. Secondly, the fact that I didn't put him in jail was premised on the idea that if he had an alcohol problem, working in the AA [Alcoholic Anonymous] organization one day a week for three years is going to give him a lot of exposure to the people with the same problem. Meanwhile, it will be helping society generally: in effect he will be making amends for his failure to pay taxes. Now that was only the second time I ever gave a sentence of that nature. On one prior occasion when I was sitting as the visiting judge, I had a dentist who had been convicted of insurance fraud. He had stood trial before another judge once, and it had been a hung jury. Before me, he was convicted, but I must say the government's case wasn't overwhelming. It was a close case. Needless to say, insurance fraud is a very heinous thing. I was torn between giving him jail time and not giving him jail time and I finally settled on giving him an alternative; I sentenced him to six months in jail, but if he chose to he could work one day a week as a volunteer dentist. Needless to say he selected the part of being a volunteer dentist. Those were the two sentences in which I gave what you might call an alternative kind of time.

INTERVIEWER: You didn't feel you needed to mete out a prison sentence for these cases in order to achieve general deterrence?

JUDGE: In both instances I thought you could make an argument that deterrence called for a sentence and in both instances, I was reluctant. The lawyer . . . I don't think too many people knew about this situation. But the dentist case was a big thing and I was conscious of the generally unfavorable reaction that should come from not getting jail time for being involved in the crime, and I hoped to offset that somewhat by giving the alternate sentence so that if you stop and view it, I would guess that a dentist makes in the area of $50 an hour eight hours a day; that is $400 dollars a day. He in effect was going to contribute sixty thousand dollars worth of services before he was done and that is not chicken feed. So you are right, there is good argument to be made from the other side and I certainly gave substantial consideration to it, I think you have to view the deterrent aspect in every sentence.

That the community service sentence is generally dependent on the offender's abilities and that it is unequally available to the total pool of offenders was emphasized in the additional comments of the judge in comparing a master's degree defendant (Mr. A) with a securities fraud defendant (Mr. B).

INTERVIEWER: Let's say that Mr. B had come up with a program to work full-time in a charitable organization. There certainly is a vast difference between going to prison and being able to go home at night. Would that not have been an appropriate sentence given what you said about Mr. A?

JUDGE: Well, it is hard to talk hypothetically because we are not dealing with hypothetical people, we are dealing with real people. Mr. B could not have come up with an alternative, (1) because of his age, (2) because he was a very sick man, (3) because of the fact that he did not have anything comparable to offer to society except the business of making money by putting together schemes. He was a business broker. The other man had a master's in social work and was an excellent worker in his job. Did a phenomenal job at that office.

Though we do not have a direct measure of frequency, there is a widespread belief that the number of community service dispositions is increasing rapidly. We obtained the same impression from our interviews. A good example of this came from a judge who had sentenced executives in two major corporate prosecutions in the last five years. In the more recent case, in which sentences were imposed about six months before our interview, he gave community service dispositions. Yet four years earlier he gave prison sentences to executives who were convicted of the same crime in nearly the exact circumstances. When asked what explained the difference, he said;

The first time around I didn't have the community disposition before me as an alternative. I simply didn't think of it. In the case I sentenced last year the attorneys met with me several times, presented a detailed program of alternative services, and convinced me that I should give it a try. So far it has worked. Had this same program been presented to me five years ago I might have used it then, . . . though the atmosphere is different today, too. I don't know.

The Problem of Special Sensitivity
and Judicial Empathy

With regard to all of the considerations of consequences, especially those associated with arguments that the process is punishment enough, there is one shadowy consideration that troubles many judges. That is the possibility that they will treat white-collar offenders differently because they can empathize with their plight. Being able more easily to identify with them, they may be prone to leniency.

The empathy factor leads some judges to compare the prison environment to the environment from which the defendant comes in order to determine whether imprisonment is an appropriate sentence. One judge put it this way:

> There is no getting away from the fact that the type of existence that jail provides is more hard on people who are accustomed to the better existence than it is on people who may not be fed as well in their homes as they are in jail. That is something you really can't articulate. It sounds as though you are penalizing poverty. There is no question that that is a fact. A person who doesn't get three square meals a day, and no possibility of getting it, isn't so seriously hurt by being put in an environment where at least you are to get three meals a day, regardless of what other disadvantages there are, than one who is in the habit of—he is just deprived of—gets no benefit from it—all deprivation. But you can't articulate that. It sounds condescending—but it has to be a factor. . . . I guess there is no getting away from the fact that the judge empathizes more with a white-collar person whose hardships you can understand, because a life style is more like his or her own, than someone whose life style you really can't understand.

The reference to empathy was not peculiar or limited to one judge. Part of the difficulty and the difference of sentencing white-collar offenders is that judges recognize that the life of the offender is not terribly different from that of the judge or people the judge knows. As one judge put it in discussing an embezzlement case,

> It was a very difficult case to sentence, I found. The most difficult kind of case to sentence are the cases where people like you are standing in front of you. That you relate to. And this was a woman who is—comes from a social structure similar to mine, I suppose, I don't know her at all, but I suppose with a background, an educated background, a job, a professional job, clean, pretty, well-dressed. You don't see yourself there, you see your wife there, you see your daughter there, something like that you know—it's very difficult at that time to stand off and be objective. You really have to steel yourself to do it.

Or, as other judges suggested,

Probably the most important factor in sentencing in cases of white-collar crime is the empathy factor. Most of the judges in this district are white and middle class. When they see a white-collar defendant they no doubt say to themselves, "There, but for the grace of God, go I."

Sentencing white-collar offenders, it is a more emotional experience. Yes, the emotions were on fire when I say—even if I say sixty days. I feel more of an emotional tug as to say to that guy thirty days, sixty days. You see the impact on him. He has never thought of going to jail in his life. It is much more emotional to him, and you can't help but be aware of that. Whereas the guy that comes in twenty two years old and he has passed a couple of bad checks and he is going to do sixty days, you know I am not saying jail is pleasant for him, it isn't. But I don't think it is the same emotional experience to him and I don't think you get the empathy from the judge because of what is happening with the individual.

I'm aware that a six-month sentence for white-collar defendants can be a major disruption for the family, for the individual. It may undermine his whole career. I guess it is true that I can probably understand better the white-collar defendant. He is more like me and that probably—I guess I do believe that white-collar defendants are more sensitive to and more affected by a prison experience. It is not the same when you have been in and out of prison three or four times and you come out of these crime-ridden communities.

Judicial empathy separates the sentencing of white- and non-white-collar criminals, and it is also believed by some judges to account for what they say are systematic differences in sentences:

> INTERVIEWER: But let us compare first offenders in the nonviolent blue-collar area and the white-collar area. You are saying that the people in the blue-collar area get more hard sentences? If you compare a first offender in both of these areas, why is that?
> JUDGE: Well, I don't know why that is. One explanation is that the judges are able to identify more readily with white-collar criminals than they are with blue-collar criminals.
> INTERVIEWER: It was identifying.
> JUDGE: With white-collar criminals. That is one allegation. Or

because they are middle-class people, the judge is able to relate to them. He can see himself in their position. Because he had the same kind of background, the same nice wife and three kids living in a nice suburb, and how terrible if that man goes to jail. That is one explanation. Whereby somebody who lives in the South Bronx who never had a job and left his wife and deserted his three children, right away he is a different individual and that might affect the judge's view and usually the defendant is sentenced for what he is, not what he did. I think that is true about our sentencing system.

This was the one area in our interviewing where judges were self-consciously aware of the possible effects of the defendant's status on their capacity to administer impartial justice. Whether this special sensitivity leads to a bias in sentencing outcomes is a question we cannot answer. A judge may identify with a defendant, yet sentence according to principle, indeed, may "lean over backward" to do so. We return to this issue in our concluding chapter.

It is clear that those who sit in judgment are deeply concerned with calculating the likely effects of the sentences they impose. The judges we interviewed neither begin nor end as pure utilitarians, but utilitarians they are nevertheless. As they think and talk about the sentencing of white-collar crime offenders one cannot help being struck by the complexity, subtlety, and, often, duality of the factors they consider.

So strong is the belief in deterrence that in most white-collar cases incarceration is a likely possibility, even if the defendant has no prior record. Deterrence often leads judges to consider prison in white-collar cases in which judgments of harm and blameworthiness would not, in themselves, justify it.

This belief is offset by a clear acknowledgment of the importance of other factors, most of which pull in the direction of a less severe sentence. The white-collar defendant, more than his common crime counterpart, can facilitate compensation and make reparations to the community he has offended. As judges view it, he is more likely to deserve special consideration on grounds of age and health, and his very status as a white-collar person means that he has already suffered much from the exposure indictment brings. Furthermore, because of his position in the world of work and family, his incarceration will cause harm to others. When these factors are joined with the non-criminal record of most white-collar defendants, they become a powerful endorsement for a nonincarcerative sentence.

Thus we are struck by the fundamental tension many judges feel between the aims of general deterrence on the one hand and the particular attributes of white-collar offenders on the other. This tension is expressed in a variety of ways, but part of its centrality is suggested in another quotation from one of our judges:

> The problem is the tension between use of incarceration for its deterrent factor, and the inclination not to use it because it is too excessive, given the noncriminal record of the offender. From the individual standpoint there are good arguments against sentencing; from the societal interest of deterring crime there are some good arguments for using the sentence. And that tension is more pronounced with the white-collar criminal, who by and large has in my judgment no prior record so that his personal interests are in his favor but the crimes he has committed I tend to think, are the ones that are deterred by sentences more so than the bad check guys and the other guys where I don't think there is much deterrent effect by incarceration. So the deterrent effect I think is at its highest, the personal situation rather favorable, and so the tension between those two values is very acute.

In seeking to resolve this conflict, many judges appear to look for a compromise: a sentence that will have what they perceive to be a deterrent effect, but that does not impose the deprivations that would come from an extended stay in prison. The weekend sentence, the short jail term, and the use of amended sentences (in which a judge imposes a prison term and later reduces it) are evidence of this search for a compromise.

In discussions of the sentencing of common crime defendants, incapacitation and rehabilitation are often mentioned as goals. The general view among the judges is that incapacitation simply is not a serious concern in white-collar cases. Keeping white-collar offenders from repeating their crimes is not like keeping a murderer or rapist from attacking yet another victim. White-collar crimes do not have the kind of impact that requires incapacitation. In fact, by virtue of arrest and conviction, most white-collar offenders are removed from the occupational setting in which their crimes were made possible. One need not put them behind bars in order to protect society from them, though one may put them there for other reasons.

Similarly, even though some judges have more faith in rehabilitation than many current theorists, they do not believe it is needed in white-collar cases. The white-collar offender, in their view, really does not need vocational training or special counseling. Most are unlikely to repeat their crimes anyway.

But considerations other than the usually discussed aims and purposes of sentencing do feed into the judges' decision-making process. These considerations would rarely be thought of as primary aims of sanctioning, but they often appear to play a primary role. In carrying out their task judges seem to develop their own "common law" standard. One implicit rule might be formulated as follows: Sentence so as to reduce the total social cost of the offense to its victims. This leads to sentences that will facilitate victim compensation and reparations. Another implicit rule would appear to be: Sentence so as not to harm innocent parties. This leads to sentences that keep the offender in the home and at work. These and perhaps other implicit principles appear to weigh heavily in the judges' decisions.

The judges, however, rarely formulate these considerations as aims or principles of sentencing. Rather, they arise as practical matters of concern in particular cases. If anything, there would appear to be a predilection against the formulation of abstract sentencing principles and a strongly felt need to keep the process oriented to the individuals who are most affected by it. This is one reason for their interest in alternative sentences that bring the offender into some relationship with the victim or the community.

In sentencing white-collar offenders, judges are torn between leniency and severity. While deterrence pulls judges in the direction of incarceration, consideration of the effects of incarceration on the offender and on his immediate social network pulls in the opposite direction. When these tensions are added to the considerations of harm and of blame, we can begin to see how complex the judges' task becomes.

■ 6

Making Sense of Sentencing

Our research was conducted against the backdrop of a common understanding that there is, in the United States, great disparity in the sentences given to offenders committing similar offenses when they appear before different judges. The common understanding suggests that there are few or no principles of sentencing, with most of the work of decision making falling to the personal preferences and individual ideologies of judges throughout the country. This situation is caused, it is argued, by the absence of strict statutory rules or case precedent upon which judges might rely in making decisions. Broad discretion has led, it is said, to lawlessness in sentencing.

In conducting our research, we asked judges to talk in detail about cases in which they had acted as the sentencing judge. We did this in order to learn how they think about sentencing and how they decide particular cases. Our interviews indicate that, far from lawlessness, there is substantial consensus about the characteristics of offenses and offenders that are important in assessing the seriousness of a crime as well as general agreement about the results judges want to achieve in meting out sentences. The regularity with which judges speak about a determinate group of factors reflecting seriousness of crime and appropriateness of sentence suggests strongly that there is a patterned system of sentencing among judges: a kind of informal common law of sentencing.

The factors to which judges routinely attend—harm, blameworthiness, and consequence—are deeply rooted in Anglo-American legal culture. When judges make sentencing decisions, they draw on principles that have traditionally provided foundations for the criminal law and have established the conditions for determination of guilt. They contain the fundamental ideas about the area of law of which sentencing is a part: the substantive criminal law and criminal law theory.

The three factors reflect a more rational and principle-bound sentencing process than is often recognized, a process in which judges spend substantial time identifying and assessing multiple indicators of seriousness of crime and appropriateness of sentence. We did not find much evidence of judges whose decisions were grounded on impressionistic judgments or based on broad generalizations, nor judges who routinely sought mechanical equality through application of rigid rules. The process of deciding on a sentence appears to involve a reasonably careful analysis of a complex event and a multifaceted offender. Judges do substantive justice through sentencing: their special ways of achieving this end are related to the absence of much explicit substantive sentencing law. In its absence, they draw less upon their own individual biases than upon a body of cultural norms quite thoroughly institutionalized in our society. To a considerable degree, sentencing is both rational and principled beneath its appearance of lawlessness.[1]

But here we have a major problem. In spite of the rationality and principled basis of sentencing, there remains substantial variability in actual sentences. Judges who talk in similar general terms often come to different judgments, in particular cases, about whether or not to imprison or for how long. The road from general principles to specific, concrete sentences is fraught with bumps and potholes. Why?

Disparity in the Face of Consensus: The Problem of Getting to a Specific Sentence

In order to get to a specific sanction a judge must complete three critical judgment tasks: (1) measure the extent to which each of his general concerns with harm, blameworthiness, and consequence is present in the particular case, (2) determine the relative weight of each factor in order to establish a summary measure that

---

1. This is not the place to explore in depth the sources of the common values expressed by our judges. Those sources include, as is implicit in our discussion, the inheritance of a common sociolegal culture, but they undoubtedly also include the fact that most judges participate in a more immediate legal culture surrounding law schools and bar association meetings. And of course there are sentencing councils and sentencing institutes that address these matters directly. These forces may tend to offset any differences in background, temperament, and style that judges bring to their work.

takes account of their being multiple factors, and (3) translate the combined measure of factors into a specific sentence.

Despite there being broad agreement on the basic principles, there is little evidence that different judges employ the same methods of measuring harm, blameworthiness, and consequence, weighting these factors, or translating them into a specific disposition. In fact, it is difficult to determine just how judges combined factors in making assessments of different aspects of the same case. We suggest that there is an important difference between the task of identifying the basic factors guiding sentencing decisions, about which there is much agreement, and the task of measuring, weighting, and combining those factors into a specific disposition.

The Problems of Measurement, Weighting, and Combining

Consider harm. There is overwhelming agreement that harm is relevant and important; there is even agreement about what the indicators of harm are, namely, money damage, duration of offense, type of victimization, and extent of violation of trust. There is not similar agreement when judges attempt to measure the separate indicators. In an embezzlement case, for example, a judge may think of monetary damages as being equivalent to profit gained by the defendant, to direct loss to the victim, to consequential loss to the victim (like lost opportunities), or to loss to the public coffers. To take another example, seriousness of victimization may be measured by the numbers of victims, the helplessness of victims, the socioeconomic status of victims, or the total dollars lost through victimization.

In cases where breach of trust is at issue, one judge may regard as most serious the breach of trust with individual victims (as in some land fraud cases), while another may feel more strongly about the breach of fiduciary trust; or one may feel that breach of public trust is equally as serious as breach of private trust, while another may regard breach of public trust as deserving of a much harsher penalty.

The matter of fitting a sentence to a case is further complicated when a judge is forced to weigh multiple forms of harm. How much breach of trust, one asks, is equivalent to significant money damage? How does a judge form an overall measure of harm from the various separate indicators of harm?

The same problems arise in connection with the dimensions of blameworthiness and consequence. Greed, cover-up, schemingness, behavior prior to indictment, and behavior from indictment to sentence are all indicators of blameworthiness. But each provides its own distinctive problems of measurement. And this is followed by the problem of weighting: how much greed is serious greed calling for a more serious appraisal of the crime? How much cooperation or remorse is needed in order to reduce the overall degree of seriousness?

In respect to consequence, judges must ask themselves, how do I measure the potential effect of the sentence on the offender? What will be the deterrent effect of a sentence on the type of potential offenders represented by the specific offender that stands before me? How do I assess the effect of the sentence on persons dependent on the offender? And again there is the problem of combining factors. Different judges weigh differently an expected high deterrent effect of a prison sentence against, for instance, the heavy loss experienced by a defendant in legal fees and administrative and business-place sanctions. How costs to family members and other dependents are combined with the other consequence factors is similarly difficult to specify.

These problems, it must be emphasized, are even more apparent across dimensions than within them. One judge thinks that more importance should be given to the blameworthiness dimension, while another emphasizes harm; a third may concentrate on the consequence of the sentence on the offender, while a fourth may stress the general deterrent effect.[2] Dissensus in sentencing, then, stems importantly from different methods of measuring, weighting, and combining. Judges tend to agree on *what* deserves weight at time of sentencing, but not on *how much* weight it deserves.

The Problem of Translating to a Specific Sentence

How do considerations of harm, blameworthiness, and consequence translate into an actual sentence? Assume that all judges did use the same factors, measured them identically, and weighed and combined them in the same way. Even if such uniformity were achieved, there

---

2. The deterrent effect, however, is most likely to be considered within limits imposed by considerations of harm and blameworthiness. See below.

might still be substantial dissensus about fitting a sentence to a crime. One judge's scale for a prison sentence may start from a minimum of two months while another judge's may start from a minimum of six months. One judge may choose jail over no jail just a little way up the scale of seriousness, while another may require greater harm or blame before sending a person to prison. This translation process is further complicated by the fact that different judges employ different units of time. A more serious case may lead to a stiffer sentence, but one judge may think in units of one month, while another may think in units of three months.

One manifestation of this translation problem is seen when judges in one federal district assign sentences proportionally different from judges handling similar cases in another district. The variance is largely due to different translations of seriousness in one district compared to another. In the sentencing of federal white-collar offenders, this discrepancy is evident in a comparison of sentences in the northern district of Texas (mainly Dallas) with those in the southern district of New York (mainly Manhattan and the Bronx). The Texas sentences are significantly more harsh across a range of white-collar crimes.[3] Thus, while judges evaluate the relative seriousness of cases similarly they may have different cutting points for determining which offenders go to prison and which do not.

Relation to Current Thought

These joint problems of measurement, weighting, and combining, on the one hand, and translation to a specific sentence, on the other, are of course hardly new to the criminal justice system. Indeed, they have received much recent attention.[4] We think it important, however, that these problems, serious though they are, be seen against the background of the considerable degree of consensus on the most basic

3. Stanton Wheeler, David Weisburd, and Nancy Bode, "Sentencing the White Coller Offender: Rhetoric and Reality," *American Sociological Review* 47 (1982):641–59. See also John Hagen, Ilene H. Nagel, and Celesta Albonetti, "The Differential Sentencing of White Collar Offenders in the Federal Courts," *American Sociological Review* 45 (1980):802–20.

4. Andrew von Hirsh addresses the problems in roughly similar terms, referring to the former as the problem of obtaining consensus on "ordinal magnitude" and the latter as the problem of "cardinal magnitude," or how to "anchor" the judgments of relative harm and blameworthiness to an actual structure or scale of penalties (see von Hirsch, *Past or Future Crimes* [Rutgers University Press, 1985], chap. 4).

norms underlying the system. If one offender gets probation and another goes to prison because of disagreements over the weighting of different types of harm, or the relative weight to be given blameworthiness or consequence, or over the translation of a given level of wrongdoing into an actual number, there is a problem to be sure, but it is not a problem of total lawlessness in sentencing. Rather, it suggests a lack of uniformity in the application of complex and sensitive criteria for sentencing.[5]

A different way of expressing the problem is to focus on the general versus the particular. If judges agree on generalities but disagree on details, those disagreements will produce disparate sentences. There may be major differences over the precise weighting of desert-based considerations relative to deterrence, or between the general and specific deterrence issues raised in chapter 5. But the rather considerable consensus on issues of harm and culpability, and more generally on what deserves weight, convinces us that much of the variability in sentencing stems from these narrow problems of measurement and translation, problems that are difficult, to be sure, but not insurmountable.

Our findings seem quite consistent with those of a psychologist who has examined these issues carefully. Diamond, who has explored sources of disparity in studies of federal judges, notes "substantial consistency in the variables that appear to determine sentence levels," and in the direction of their effects.[6] The judges do disagree, however, on the weights to be given each factor, and panels of three judges giving independent sentencing judgments on a case disagreed over whether custody should be imposed 30 percent of the time. In further

5. These problems are analogous to those facing people with complex weighting and choice options in other spheres, and for which public choice theory has developed models. For an application to courts and administrative agencies, see Matthew L. Spitzer, "Multicriteria Choice Processes: An Application of Public Choice Theory to Bakke, the F.C.C., and the Courts," 88 *Yale Law Journal* 717–79 (March 1979). On the related problem of information processing in consumer choice situations, see David M. Grether, Alan Schwartz, and Louis L. Wilde, "The Irrelevance of Information Overload: An Analysis of Search and Disclosure," 59 *Southern California Law Review* 277–303 (January 1986).

6. Shari Seidman Diamond, "Exploring Sources of Disparity," in *The Trial Process*, ed. Bruce Dennis Sales (New York: Plenum, 1981), 405. A communication to the authors from Jerry L. Mashaw, an administrative law specialist who has studied the workings of discretion in workmen's compensation and social security settings, finds the Diamond findings and ours good evidence that the variance in sentences is modest for systems dealing with judgmental issues.

examining the sources of disparity in those cases where judges disagreed, Diamond noted two types of cases likely to be found with some frequency in white-collar crimes: those with a mixture of mitigating and aggravating factors and those in which there is "a single characteristic that suggests both high culpability and a good prognosis."[7] As we noted in chapter 4, many white-collar offenders combine "blameworthy status" and "praiseworthy conduct" in a way that complicates the judicial decision, and it would seem to be those kinds of cases that are most likely to produce inconsistent outcomes.

The differential weighting of diverse principles of sentencing raises both philosophical and practical problems. Indeed, in recent years perhaps the major sentencing issue has been how to harmonize desert-based thinking (roughly our harm and blameworthiness dimensions) with utilitarianism (roughly our consequence dimension).[8] And Robinson has noted how the listing of conventional punishment goals does little to help decide when one or another should prevail at sentencing.[9] Quite a number of years ago, however, H. L. A. Hart had already given his seminal lecture to the Aristotelian Society in which he showed that neither a pure utilitarian nor a pure retributive theory of punishment could possibly claim to give a complete explanation of why and when society punishes with the criminal law; thus he argued that there must be a theoretical integration of utilitarian and retributive ideas.[10]

Blameworthiness, as used by the judges, is most closely associated with a just deserts, or retributive, theory of punishment. Is it *justified*, our judges would often ask, to punish this defendant? In this sense, the blameworthiness measure acts as a break on or a precondition to the meting out of punishment for utilitarian *aims*. In other contexts in our interviews, however, a utilitarian theme comes through in the blameworthiness factor. Judges want to punish the more devious and more morally depraved offenders more

7. Shari Seidman Diamond, "Order in the Court: Consistency in Criminal-Court Decisions," in *The Master Lecture Series*, vol. 2: *Psychology and the Law*, ed. C. T. Schriever and B. L. Hammond (New York: American Psychological Association, 1983), 136.

8. Paul H. Robinson, "Hybrid Principles for the Distribution of Criminal Sanctions" (Paper delivered at Yale Law School Seminar, March 27, 1986).

9. *Ibid.*

10. The year was 1959. See chap. 1, "Prolegomenon to the Principles of Punishment," *Punishment and Responsibility* (Oxford: Oxford University Press, 1968).

harshly because their behavior needs to be suppressed more fully. In the field of white-collar crime, the nature of the injury, in the Beccarian sense of injury to society, is often a function of the wrongdoer's mental state. Society is injured more by a business-person who violates trust in a calculated and scheming manner than it is by a person who violates trust in response to overwhelming situational pressures. In this way, blameworthiness measures have also become criteria of injury to society and therefore utilitarianlike measures of consequent punishment.

The striking thing to us is that the judges we interviewed, unlike the current commentators, seemed relatively unconcerned about whether they labeled their sentencing desert-oriented or utilitarian and deterrence-oriented. Perhaps because we asked about concrete cases rather than abstract sentencing goals, we received direct responses about what it is in the offender, the offense, and the effect of the punishment that makes a difference to the judges, rather than general statements about conflicts between different purposes of sentencing. The advantage in our methodology is in its breaking through abstract philosophical talk to concrete criteria. What is important is that judges distinguish clearly between harm, blameworthiness, and consequence. It means little to them whether one labels their concern with harm or blameworthiness as tied to a retributive theory of sentencing or tied to a utilitarian theory of sentencing. This does not mean, however, that judges are unconcerned with the values underlying retributive or utilitarian theories of punishment. These values would certainly be identified by judges were they asked to give general justifications for the criminal sanction. But the actual sentencing process, as we have tried to show, is steeped in the conventional language of the criminal law, not in the language of theory.

Perhaps a central lesson to be drawn from our judges is that sentencing law must focus directly on judge-relevant categories like the ones we have defined here, while steering away from any applied use of terms like *utilitarianism* and *just deserts*. While these broad concepts may constitute philosophical underpinnings of the system of criminal law and punishments, the instruments judges need in sentencing are narrower concepts that can be translated into identifiable characteristics of cases.

When we focus our analysis on the core measures—harm, blameworthiness, and consequence—rather than on philosophies of punishment, we are convinced that despite some exceptions, judges do share a common body of thought, some of it distinctively legal but much of it institutionalized in the commonsense moral judgments that are found throughout our society. The same general consensus tends to be found when the public is asked for its judgments about the relative seriousness of different crimes.[11] This reinforces our view that a rational sentencing system reflecting the judgments of our common social order is not a hopeless dream. The question is not whether but how? What concrete steps can be taken to bring us closer to a system of sentencing in which agreements on principle can be translated into equal treatment for similar cases?

Improving the System in a World without Guidelines

The guidelines movement is the current proposed solution to the problems posed by sentencing disparities, but before we examine the relevance of our findings for federal sentencing guidelines, we should note needed changes that are in some measure independent of the guidelines movement.

The Need for a Richer Jurisprudence of Sentencing

The first and most apparent need is for a jurisprudence of sentencing that will bring the work of the moral and legal philosopher closer to the problems faced by judges at time of sentencing. Although the roots of sentencing are deeply embedded in the culture, there are many points at which a coherent jurisprudence of sentencing is lacking, with resulting ambiguity and confusion. Examples abound. With respect to assessments of social harm, for example, what monetary figures should guide us in assessing the crime of bribery? Is the critical ingredient the amount paid to the bribee? Or should it be the amount (presumably much larger) that will be netted by the briber? Without a more developed jurisprudence of bribery (part of a more general

11. Alfred Blumstein and Jacqueline Cohen, "Sentencing of Convicted Offenders: An Analysis of the Public's View," 14 *Law and Society Review* 223 (1980). Further evidence that the judges are not alone in their views comes from the various federal and state parole and sentencing guidelines that often list factors like those the judges named—trust violation, relative culpability, role of ringleaders vs. less central figures—as legitimate bases for aggravating or mitigating the penalties.

jurisprudence of harm) sentencing judges may have to fall back on their own devices, for these are not matters clearly spelled out in the common culture. Similarly, we lack clear guidelines for assessing the relative culpability of a low-level public official who accepts a bribe and a high-level private businessman who offers one. Does the holding of *any* form of public office create obligations that exceed those applying to *any* private party?

This example leads into a more general consideration of the jurisprudence of blame. What are the justifications for a system in which judges are invited to make moral judgments about the offender's conduct not only at the time of the crime, but both before and after? Are there principled bases for asserting the relative importance of the judgments of character based on the defendent's prior life, his role and mental state during the commission of the offenses in question, or his behavior vis-à-vis authorities in the period between indictment and sentence? As we showed in chapter 4, judges consider many points all the way along the defendant's career and argue that each may be relevant for the sentencing decision. This is only one of the many questions we are left with in the as-yet-incomplete jurisprudence of blame.

When we come to the jurisprudence of consequence, there is an extraordinary set of questions to be addressed. Is there principled justification for giving weight to the effects of the sentence on the offender's social circle, or is it enough to say, as some judges do, that the offender "should have thought about them" before committing the offense? And what if the defendant's circle includes many who are dependent on the defendant's company for employment and who will be out of work if the company closes?

Those who must decide these moral and judgmental issues would be greatly aided in their efforts if more thoughtful assessments were available to them.[12] But if philosophical efforts are to be of value, they must be addressed to the real problems judges face. Their audience would have to be the practitioners of justice,

12. In some areas, steps have been taken toward such a jurisprudence: Andrew von Hirsh on how to think about prior record, Joel Feinberg on conceptualizing harm, and Kip Schlegel on the allocation of punishment to corporations are three recent examples. See von Hirsh, *Past or Future Crimes*; Joel Feinberg, *Harm to Others: The Moral Limits of Our Criminal Law* (New York: Oxford University Press, 1987); Kip Schlegel, "Desert and the Allocation of Punishment for Corporations and Their Agents" (Ph.D. diss., Rutgers University, 1987).

rather than its other priests. A closer dialogue between those who do justice and those who write about it would be beneficial to both.

Coming to Terms with the Issues of Measurement and Weighting

The criminal justice system cannot wait for the emergence of a refined jurisprudence of sentencing to solve its problems. In the meantime, are there some practical steps that might be taken to deal with the disparities that exist in the measurement and weighting of sentencing variables?

When we look solely at the measurement problem *within* a particular dimension of sentencing, for example, the various measures of harm, it is possible that the problems are less severe than they may appear. The various indicators of harm may be highly intercorrelated, so that differences in judicial preferences for one or the other may have little practical effect. In the traditions of social science methodology, there is a doctrine of the "inter-changeability of indicators,"[13] a way of referring to the fact that of several different ways of measuring, say, social status, it may turn out that they all bear about the same relationship to whatever it is social status predicts. If, for example, the dollar amount of a fraud is much larger for those frauds that continue over a period of years, then whether one judge stresses the duration while another stresses the size, the practical result will be the same. It is only when we contrast the theft of small amounts over a long period with the one-time offense of gigantic proportions that the two judges might sentence in very different ways. Again, this is not to say that there is *no* problem—only that the problem may arise infrequently.

There is a different problem with the various indicators of blameworthiness, especially when we contrast those that arise prior to or during an offense with those that arise after. For it is precisely those who were most involved, or whose pasts give little reason to expect sympathy from a judge, who may have the most to gain from cooperating with the authorities and/or giving the appearance of remorse. We think that as a practical matter, judges must come to a clearer

13. Hortense Horowitz and Elias Smith, "The Interchangeability of Socio-Economic Indices," in *The Language of Social Research*, ed. Paul Lazarsfeld and Morris Rosenberg (Glencoe, Ill.: Free Press, 1955), 73–77.

sense of what they are doing in the calculus of blame when they give major discounts for those who cooperate with authorities. Some cooperation is often treated as a sign of repentance and emergent prosocial behavior, when it is more likely an effort to save one's own skin. The law enforcement community may rightly urge such cooperation as the only way to bring others to justice, but discussing the issue in those terms would at least focus attention not on the morality or psychology of the criminal but on the question, How much should the norms and principles of sentencing be bent in order to meet the needs of law enforcement?

Finally, in the United States we have been deprived of one major source of uniformity of sentencing, namely, appellate review. In countries like England and Norway, where appellate review of sentencing is a frequent occurrence, there are judicial opinions setting forth the reasoning behind the relative weight given to one consideration or another, opinions that provide a body of written and articulated thought that, save for a few jurisdictions, is largely absent in the United States.[14] The absence is made up for in part by sentencing memoranda, often prepared by judges as they articulate the reasons for their actions. But the actions and opinions of district court judges cannot have the same binding quality on others that is true of appellate court opinions. Thus the development of appellate review of sentences might well take us a step toward greater uniformity in sentencing.[15]

Coming to Terms with the Translation Problem: The In/Out Decision and Length of Term

We are far more likely to achieve a fair degree of consensus on the relative rank ordering of offenders and their crimes than on the translation of that rank ordering into a specific in or out decision and (for those who go in) a specific length of incarceration. The choice between

14. David A. Thomas, *The Principles of Sentencing*, 2d. ed. (London: Heinemann, 1979). See also Johannes Andenaes, "The Choice of Sanction: A Scandinavian Perspective," in *Reform and Punishment: Essays on Criminal Sentencing*, ed. Michael Tonry and Franklin E. Zimring (Chicago: University of Chicago Press, 1983), 3–20.

15. But we agree with Zeisel and Diamond that appellate review can affect disparity only through effective mechanisms for feedback. See H. Zeisel and S. S. Diamond, "Search for Sentencing Equity: Sentence Review in Massachusetts and Connecticut," 4 *American Bar Foundation Research Journal* 881–940 (1977). (cited in Diamond, *Trial Process*, 410).

probation and imprisonment was perhaps a more stark one in the past than today, with the possibility of serving weekend sentences, halfway house sentences, and other way stations between the alternatives of conditional freedom and imprisonment. When justified on grounds of desert, incarceration remains the definitive expression of "the formal and solemn judgment of the moral condemnation of the community," as Henry M. Hart put it.[16] And, save for questions of incapacitation, which are rarely an issue in white-collar crimes, the imposition of incarceration on grounds of desert seems more justifiable, given our current knowledge, than on grounds of deterrence. We really need to know much more about the deterrent effects of incarceration for specific subsets of offenders if we are to get any clear notions of where the norm of consequence would help us choose between incarceration and lesser penalties.

With regard to length of term, the question How long is long? remains essentially unanswerable. Although as a practical matter one may gear sentence lengths to prison capacity, there remains a need to think through what it really means to incarcerate for different periods of time. Perhaps, however, we can get clues as to How long is long? by examining the way we deal with time in other spheres of life.

For example, for all but the very wealthy, a vacation occurs in a limited time frame—a week or two, perhaps a month at the outside. For schoolteachers and some others two- or three-month vacations are common, but for most, two to three weeks is maximum. A sentence for that same period might be likened, in terms of the feel of time if nothing else, to a vacation in that it is a brief interruption in one's normal routine and can be seen as not terribly disruptive of it. Longer periods would require a leave of absence, at least for most conventional places of work, and we should probably regard an incarcerative sentence of more than a month as having significant consequences for all but the unemployed.

Looked at differently, it takes seven to ten years of special training, counting college and graduate school, to produce most of those who occupy the highest ranking professions in our society. During that time, the trainee becomes transformed from a beginner into a thoroughly trained professional. This may happen with incarceration as

16. "The Aims of the Criminal Law," *Law and Contemporary Problems* 23, no.3 (Summer 1958):408.

well, though we should then expect to have a thoroughly trained professional thief on our hands. In any event, imprisonment for five years or more should be understood as having massive impact and should be imposed only when the combination of harm, blameworthiness, and consequence requires an extreme sanction.

The Need for Better Information

In chapter 2 we described in detail the body of information typically available to a judge at time of sentencing. Much of our attention focused on the pre-sentence investigation report (PSI), the premier document of sentencing. As we noted, the PSI was developed during a time when the rehabilitative theory of sentencing was dominant. It called for the gathering of large amounts of data on the personal background of the defendant. Although the underlying philosophy of sentencing has changed greatly, the PSI still reflects its origins. What might a reformed PSI look like if it was designed to be especially meaningful to today's sentencing judges? Again using our three major concepts as a point of orientation, we would envision a revised and reformed PSI that would have much more detailed data on the nature of the offense and on estimates of consequence, and perhaps less detail on the offender.

Current PSIs often leave unattended critical questions about the nature of the offense, including the magnitude of the crime in economic terms, the number and the nature of victims, and precise indications of the role in the crime played by the defendant relative to other parties. The PSI, after all, was supposed to be a window on the offender, not on the offense, so these gaps in current PSIs are not surprising. But judges, in our experience, are often hampered by an absence of facts on matters believed to be of critical importance in arriving at the sentence. A revised PSI would surely give more attention to the details of offense than does the current version.

Information pertaining to consequence is singularly lacking in most PSIs. This may necessarily be the case, as information on, say, the deterrent effect of this or that sanction is typically unavailable to the judge from any source, let alone the PSI. But it is possible that a creative reworking of the PSI might yield benefits for the judge. The materials on consequence are typically provided by the defendant and are likely to paint an extraordinarily sad picture of the fate to befall family and other significant losers as a result of the defendant's fall.

If consequence is to be taken as a central consideration in sentencing, we should surely do something to improve the information about consequence that flows to the sentencing judge.

Materials on the offender are of course the most detailed in the current PSI. Because of the probation officer's tie to the criminal justice system and because of his knowledge of the current status of the offender, there may actually be more detail in the PSI about the defendant's cooperation with authorities, about the show of remorse or the lack thereof, about the defendant's acceptance of guilt, than there is about the defendant's mental state at the time of the crime. Such structuring of the information may unwittingly give greater salience to the defendant's character as gleaned at the time of sentencing than to the character of the defendant as revealed at the time of the offense or before. In any event, one major consequence of changes in the philosophy of sentencing is the need for changes in the type and quality of the information available to the sentencer. Rethinking of the PSI would be a natural first step in this process.

The Guidelines Movement

The most important trend in recent sentencing reform is in the arrangement to provide guidelines for the exercise of judicial discretion in sentencing. A recent review of state legislation suggests that all fifty states have engaged in some legislative modification of their sentencing in the past ten years—a wholesale shift from earlier years.[17] While these have taken a variety of forms, the guidelines movement has achieved more recognition, comment, discussion, and study than others, and it lies at the heart of the new federal sentencing legislation. Indeed, the first task of the Federal Sentencing Commission was to establish a set of sentencing guidelines.

For a discussion of the relevance of our own data for the guidelines movement and for the establishment of Federal Sentencing Guidelines, it will help to have a specific example in front of us. The Minnesota sentencing guidelines are a natural choice, for they were based

---

17. Sandra Shane-DuBow, Alice P. Brown, and Erik Olsen, *Sentencing Reform in the United States: History, Content and Effect* (Washington: National Institute of Justice, 1985).

on much thought and research and have been described as "probably the most thoughtfully constructed statewide sentencing reform."[18]

The Minnesota system, like many others, is based upon a two-dimensional grid (table 2). A vertical axis includes ten different "severity levels of conviction offense" with unauthorized use of a motor vehicle and possession of marijuana at the low end, to murder second degree at the top. (First-degree murder is excluded from the guidelines by law, and has a mandatory life sentence in Minnesota.) The horizontal dimension expresses a criminal history score based primarily on the number of prior felony convictions, but including also the defendant's custody status at the time of conviction, some information on misdemeanors, and the juvenile record for defendants who are twenty-one years of age or younger. The basic matrix, with its bold dispositional line, distinguishes probation from incarceration sentences.[19]

The contrast between the substance of our chapters 3, 4, and 5 and the Minnesota sentencing grid suggests some of the major issues to be considered as federal authorities develop sentencing guidelines. Consider first the vertical dimension. With the important exceptions of the size of thefts and the differentiation of robberies into simple and aggravated and of assaults and murders into degrees, the issue of harm or seriousness of offense is caught up largely in the legal category of the offense itself, rather than in the kinds of qualities laid out in chapter 3. There is certainly a close parallel in the concern for the amount of monetary loss, but one misses such indicators of harm as the duration of the offense, and particularly notions of harm through violation of trust.[20]

Now as a policy matter one could argue that these factors, even though used by many sitting federal judges in their current sentencing practices, are inappropriate bases for differentiating sentences and that they should be excluded from a guidelines system. Or one could argue that they should be included, but with explicit efforts made to distinguish clearly between degrees of harm that each indicator might

---

18. Ibid., 169.
19. Reprinted from Kay A. Knapp, *Minnesota Sentencing Guidelines and Commentary Annotated* (St. Paul: Minnesota CLE Press, 1985).
20. Trust violation is included, however, as one of a number of "aggravation" reasons for major economic crimes. Ibid., 58–59.

Table 2. Minnesota Presumptive Sentence Length in Months

Criminal History Score

Severity Levels of Conviction Offense		0	1	2	3	4	5	6 or more
Unauthorized use of motor vehicle / Possession of marijuana	I	12[a]	12[a]	12[a]	15	18	21	24
Theft-related crimes ($150–$2,500) / Sale of Marijuana	II	12[a]	12[a]	14	17	20	23	27 / 25–29[b]
Theft crimes ($150–$2,500)	III	12[a]	13	16	19	22 / 21–23	27 / 25–29	32 / 30–34
Burglary-felony intent / Receiving stolen goods ($150–$2,500)	IV	12[a]	15	18	21	25 / 24–26	32 / 30–34	41 / 37–45
Simple robbery	V	18	23	27	30 / 29–31	38 / 36–40	46 / 43–49	54 / 50–58
Assault, 2nd degree	VI	21	26	30	34 / 33–35	44 / 42–46	54 / 50–58	65 / 60–70
Aggravated robbery	VII	24 / 23–25	32 / 30–34	41 / 38–44	49 / 45–53	65 / 60–70	81 / 75–87	97 / 90–104

Assault, 1st Degree Criminal sexual conduct, 1st degree	VIII	43 **41–45**	54 **50–58**	65 **60–70**	76 **71–81**	95 **89–101**	113 **106–120**	132 **124–140**
Murder, 3rd degree^c	IX	97 **94–100**	119 **116–122**	127 **124–130**	149 **143–155**	176 **168–184**	205 **195–215**	230 **218–242**
Murder, 2nd degree	X	116 **111–121**	140 **133–147**	162 **153–171**	203 **192–214**	243 **231–255**	284 **270–298**	324 **309–339**

^a One year and one day.

^b Boldface numbers denote the range within which a judge may sentence without the sentence being deemed a departure. The bold line is the dispositional line: above the line indicates probationary sentences (OUT); below the line indicates sentences of incarceration (IN).

^c First-degree murder is excluded from the guidelines by law and continues to have a mandatory life sentence.

reflect. A third solution would be to say that in the context of the federal system, with the enormous heterogeneity of actual behavior prosecuted under such statutes as those defining mail and wire fraud or bribery, more discretion simply has to be left to judges. This is not the place to argue or resolve the issues. What is important here is to note that there is a long way to travel between the approach to sentencing that currently characterizes federal judges and a system that parcels out degrees of harm largely by legal categories.

A different set of issues arises when we consider the horizontal axis—the criminal history score. That score may mean many things to different people. For some it might be regarded as a measure of relative culpability: those who commit offenses and fail to learn from their mistakes and go on to commit further offenses may be regarded as more culpable than those who are facing the criminal justice system for the first time. For others, the criminal history score may represent a rough indicator of predicted future criminality since one of the well-established facts of criminology is the tendency for offenders to repeat their crimes more often in the future the more they have committed them in the past.[21]

Thus it is necessary to decide what meaning is to be placed on the prior criminal history before we can know whether it belongs with discussion of prior record in connection with relative culpability and blameworthiness or with discussion of consequence. In the context of white-collar crime, little attention is given to the need to protect society by incarceration of particular white-collar offenders, since they are generally believed to be neither as dangerous nor as likely to repeat their offenses as are those who perpetrate the more mundane forms of common crime. But prediction of future criminality is most definitely a consequence consideration.

In either case, judges bring a much richer body of concerns to this second dimension than is reflected in even the most complex of the indicators of prior criminal history developed in guideline systems. There is little place in such systems for any of the variety of considerations relating to relative blameworthiness that were discussed in chapter 4, although some of them, it must be noted, are sometimes introduced as mitigating or aggravating circumstances. But in general

21. Alfred Blumstein et al., *Research on Sentencing: The Search for Reform* (Washington, D.C.: National Academy Press, 1983), 11.

the guideline systems permit little of the rather elaborate assessments of blameworthiness that are often found when federal judges consider the sentencing of white-collar offenders.

In many state systems, as in Minnesota, one may be able to get away with treating the major white-collar cases as falling essentially outside the guidelines system and requiring separate and special consideration.[22] That is an implausible solution in the federal system, in which a large part of the sentencing activity concerns white-collar offenses.

This raises the question of whether there can be a single set of guidelines in a system as heterogeneous as the federal system. We think there can be, but the guidelines would look very different from the current two-dimensional grid. For cases of violent crimes involving repeat offenders, violence as a measure of harm and prior record as a measure of blameworthiness or of predicted future criminality would probably receive greater weight than most of the other indicators. And where violence and prior record loom large in assessing harm and blame, then incapacitation, rarely mentioned in white-collar cases, would loom large among the measures of consequence. As part of the informal common law of sentencing, judges already draw upon these distinctions in comparing white-collar and common crimes. We think it plausible that a guidelines system could capture the main attributes federal judges now use in a much less structured way.

But the system could not remain a two-dimensional system and still do justice to the current reasoning of judges. To capture white-collar cases alone the system needs at least the three dimensions of harm, blameworthiness, and consequence, and the latter is itself a heterogeneous category. No two-dimensional grid will begin to do justice to the variety of considerations most federal judges bring to sentencing.

Common-Law Judges in an Age of Guidelines[23]

The rather extraordinary discretion at sentencing allowed by our system of justice has had to give way to a more structured, principle-bound, and rule-bound system. The prime candidate to replace rampant discretion is one or another variant of guidelines. As one moves toward such a system, it is well to keep in mind whatever wisdom a

22. See Knapp, *Minnesota Guidelines*, 58–59.
23. See Guido Calabresi, *A Common Law for the Age of Statutes* (Cambridge: Harvard University Press, 1982).

common-law system of judging might have offered if in fact there had been published opinions allowing sentencing doctrines to emerge as part of legal precedent and appellate review of sentences; in short, if there had been the same evolution of standards of judgment found in other areas of law. Each system has its strengths and weaknesses, and we should be aware of them as we engage in sentencing reform.

Common-law sentencers make qualitative judgments while guidelines sentencers count points. Common-law sentencers make individualized determinations while guidelines sentencers employ a standard set of factors. Common-law sentencers see themselves as interpretive, and their guidelines counterparts as mechanical. But guidelines sentencers view themselves as empirical and scientific, their common-law counterparts as intuitive and open to bias. Common-law sentencers are rooted in the culture, making judgments not unlike normal observers and men in the street, while guidelines sentencers are more likely to read economics and statistics and to base judgments on what they regard as scientific policy grounds.[24]

One system, using reasoned judgments, allows a multiplicity of variables and encourages attention to individual differences. The other system also uses reason and judgment, but with the aim of establishing structure and uniformity. One is more likely to treat like cases differently, while the other runs the risk of treating unlike cases alike.

The strains between these different systems of judgment are not unique to criminal sentencing. Indeed, they are likely to appear whenever there are *(a)* a large volume of cases requiring decisions, *(b)* a limited amount of time and resources to be committed to those decisions, *(c)* a commitment to fairness and equity in decision making, and *(d)* a lot riding on the outcome. When these conditions obtain, there will be pressures to establish bureaucratic procedures of the guidelines variety, and fears that the resulting guidelines will ignore individual circumstance.

The closest parallel in American law involves the procedures recently adopted for handling benefit determinations in the Social Security Administration. Decisions long made by administrative law judges were replaced by a four-factor index in which awards are based

---

24. Bruce Ackerman et al., *The Uncertain Search for Environmental Quality* (New York: Free Press, 1974). See especially chaps. 2–5; see also Charles Lindblom and David Cohen, *Usable Knowledge* (New Haven and London: Yale University Press, 1979), chap. 2.

on the applicants' combined score on items reflecting age, education, work experience, and degree of impairment. When challenged on grounds that the congressional intent had been that administrative law judges should make individual determinations and that the gridlike regulations violated the statute, the U.S. Supreme Court rejected the claim, largely on the ground that in a dispersed and far-flung system objective, standardized criteria are needed in order to produce consistency and uniformity.[25] The court saw that there were escape clauses and alternatives for cases that didn't fit the norm and approved a structure not unlike (in general outlines) a sentencing guidelines system.

Whether the sentencing of offenders in the federal system can be fairly done within the guidelines framework will depend, of course, on the particular details of the guidelines system adopted. We believe a multifactored guidelines system can work, provided it leaves room for judicial discretion within a reasonable range. A complex grid will capture most of the legitimate differences between cases but not all.

In sum, both those in the guidelines movement and common-law judges are committed to a search for more rational and consistent sentencing policies. A guidelines system like that adopted in Minnesota, developed largely to handle the mass of offenders passing through state courts, may not be easily transferable to the federal system. It will be a daunting task to develop a set of guidelines that is easy to administer and that will deal fairly and sensibly with the enormous variety of offenses and offenders entering the federal system. If it is unjust to treat like cases differently, it is also unjust to treat different cases alike. An effective guidelines system must be a delicate instrument designed to eliminate both kinds of injustice.[26]

25. Heckler v. Campbell, 461 U.S. 458 (1983). See also Jerry L. Mashaw, *Bureaucratic Justice* (New Haven and London: Yale University Press, 1983), esp. 114–21.

26. These words were written as the Federal Sentencing Commission was revising its sentencing guidelines, after these were extensively criticized for being too rigid and not allowing enough room for judicial discretion. The revisions proposed to Congress do give more leeway for individual judge discretion. The single area in which there would appear to be the greatest difference between what judges have been doing in the past and what will be expected under the guidelines is in what we call blameworthiness. Few of the considerations judges have been giving to the life history of the defendant are retained as legitimate considerations at sentencing. Among all the life history factors, for example, only criminal history is formally introduced as relevant.

Individual Differences and Organizational
. Influences: A Disclaimer

In the traditions of behavioral science, much effort goes into explaining variation, and the behavioral science of crime is no exception. Most empirical studies of sentencing are devoted to setting out correlates of length of sentence—those variables that predict whether this or that characteristic of the defendant, the official, or the system will explain why some are sentenced to more and others less.[27] Our study was not so designed, and save for what judges report about the features of defendants that influence their sentence, we have precious little to say about the subject. We know that in the practical world of criminal justice, some judges are viewed as lenient ("Turn 'em loose Bruce" and "Hit the Street Pete" come to mind) while others ("Maximum Myers") are viewed as tough sentencers. And we anticipate that even after heroic efforts are made to standardize and structure sentencing, there will remain individual differences in the way judges sentence. In our interviews we spoke with an occasional judge who articulated a special hostility toward a particular type of offender (a drug dealer in one case, a sex offender in another) based on the judge's personal experience. It would be silly to argue that those differences are not important or that (in any but the most rigid system) they will not have some influence.[28]

We also have a sense that there are individual differences in the judges' taste for principled reasoning, that some judges pursue fact-finding more aggressively than others, and that some seek more diligently than others for the appropriate sentence rationale. And as we reported in chapter 2, judges differ in how they read the indictment and the PSI. But despite these individual differences, the judges we studied did have a conception of their role *as judge*. Although there are differences in the way that role is interpreted, the judges we studied

27. Blumstein et al., *Research on Sentencing*, chapter 2; see also vol. 2, chaps. 1–3.
28. But we should not exaggerate the problem of individual differences. In the most systematic study of the problem among federal judges, Diamond found that the most severe sentences were about 10 percent above the median, while the least severe were about 10 percent below. The range of 20 percent is not to be sneezed at, but it is not the horror story that is sometimes portrayed. See Diamond, "Exploring Sources of Disparity," 403–05.

did recognize the task of judging as both different from and more demanding than the mere expression of opinion.

Just as there are individual differences, so there are influences from the broader world judges inhabit that will produce variation in sentences. Some federal districts have sentencing conferences at which judges exchange views about their cases, and in some jurisdictions there is greater attentiveness to the sentencing practices of other districts. Jurisdictions that are close to special facilities (say a new correctional treatment center or halfway house) will find their judges taking them into account in their sentencing. There is, in short, a local "courthouse culture" that is another source of variation in sentencing.

But just as it does not broach the question of individual differences, so our study is not designed to reveal organizational variation in all its complexity. To fail to study it is not to deny its existence. There is, however, some indication from our analysis that efforts to work on the problems of weighting, combining, and translating will help reduce whatever disparity owes to individual and organizational differences, or at the least will bring such disparity more clearly into view.

The Question of Generalizability

We interviewed federal district court judges, and in the interviews we focused particularly on white-collar offenders— those convicted of tax fraud, securities fraud, postal and wire fraud, bank embezzlement, bribery, and similar violations of federal law. Would we have found anything similar had we concentrated on so-called common crimes? Although we cannot know for sure, we have the strong sense that our findings may not be as different as some might imagine. Indeed, as our discussion of the possibility of a single guidelines system implies, we believe there is in practice an implicit common law of sentencing that gives expression to a widely shared set of principles.

Consider first the question of the court system. It is undoubtedly true that federal judges have more resources at their disposal than do most state court judges and that they typically do not have the same time pressures and calendar pressures that often plague the work of state sentencers in state court systems. Thus we would expect federal judges to have greater time for making subtle distinctions between offenders and perhaps a more thorough assessment of alternatives and of the underlying rationale for the sentence imposed. But studies of the lower criminal courts suggest that factors very similar to those we have discussed come into play in the sentencing of common crime defendants. When Feeley assessed the sentencing of defendants in the lower criminal courts of New Haven, he was struck that judgments of the appropriate "going rate" were based on assessments, crude to be sure, of harm, blame, and consequence not unlike the factors we have found in federal cases of white-collar crime.[29] Judgments may be made more crudely, and in a bargain basement atmosphere, but prosecutors and judges in the lower criminal courts seem to be employing a logic not unlike that found in the cases we studied.

Such a finding should not be surprising, for the general legal culture out of which the central concepts flow contributes both to the stream of cases that wind up in the federal courts and to those that inhabit the lower reaches of state court systems. The same legal culture has within it both white-collar and common crime elements. The comparison suggests, if anything, the similarity of the processes and categories rather than their differences.

When we turn to the nature of the crime instead of the court, a basically similar picture emerges. We cannot know for sure, for the relevant detailed research has not been done, but discussions of sentencing among a wide range of federal and state judges suggests to us that here too the similarities outweigh the differences.

What if we had studied persons convicted of bank robbery, drug offenses, or assault instead of the white-collar crimes we examined? With regard to each of our major dimensions, we think we would have found some differences, but some important similarities. With respect to harm, for example, the amount of the take, the duration of involvement, and the presence of an identifiable victim are likely to aggravate the sentence for common crime defendants just as they do for white-collar offenders. Judges may give somewhat less attention to the magnitude of the offense in monetary terms, if that magnitude is likely to depend on the accident of what the victim was carrying at

29. Malcolm Feeley, *The Process Is the Punishment* (New York: Russell Sage, 1979).

the time of the robbery rather than on the more careful calculus of many white-collar offenders. This discrepancy, however, goes not to the presence of the factor but to its weight.

We would have found much more detailed attention to assessments of the harm involved in attacks upon the person—the relative harm emerging from the threat of force as against its actual use, from being knocked down as against being beaten or stabbed. We would surely have gotten a more refined sense for the calculus of physical harm, as the judges see it, than we did by concentrating on white-collar offenses. But that really suggests the universality of the process. Just as there appears to be an informal common law of harm for white-collar crimes, so there is an informal common law of harm for common crimes.

Similarly, many of the elements of blameworthiness apply equally to white-collar and common crime defendants: whether they play a central or peripheral role in the offense, whether the offense was carefully and rationally planned, whether their prior life consisted mainly of good or bad deeds, whether they engaged in cover-up or showed remorse for their offense, whether there was greed or need—all of these elements are found in the crimes committed by violent offenders as well as in those committed by white-collar criminals. We probably would have found a much more richly articulated sense of the meaning of prior record than with the mostly first offender population of white-collar defendants. Yet this suggests only that each type of offense may have its own position in the matrix of blameworthiness, not that the processes of thought and judgment are dissimilar.

With respect to consequence, we anticipate that notions of deterrence and of general prevention are given much more play in white-collar cases and that the relatively refined calculus relating to the occupational status of the offender which we detail in chapter 5 reaches its finest flowering in white-collar cases and will be treated more crudely in common crime deliberations. Conversely, in common crimes, especially those involving violence, notions of incapacitation will be central. But our main point is that what would change is the depth of detail and the richness of the indicators for the various aspects of consequence. The general categories and the process of judgment about them may well be similar across the range of crimes and offenders.

We believe, then, that there is evidence of a kind of implicit general theory of sentencing in what the judges do. The general theory is incomplete, to be sure, especially in providing for systematic weighting and combining of the dimensions and in translating the weighting into a specific in/out decision or length of sentence. It is at these key points, as we have emphasized, that organizational factors and individual differences have their impact. While the dissensus in sentencing is surely in part the dissensus inherent in any discretionary system of decision making, a fully developed theory of sentencing would enlarge the area of principled consensus.

There was one major exception to this general conclusion. As we noted in chapter 5 and as we have detailed elsewhere,[30] judges often show a special sensitivity to white-collar offenders. The white-collar offender may remind the judge of a colleague or neighbor, while the street offender is no more than a stranger. This may make it easier to conclude that one offender is more deserving of probation than the other. In a fully articulated sentencing system, this exception would be reduced. The important thing about any given case would be where the crime and criminal are located on the general dimensions of harm, blameworthiness, and consequence—dimensions that apply to common as well as to white-collar crimes.

We began our research with an interest in how federal district court judges make their fateful sentencing decisions. We did not begin with a theory that we were going to put to test. Of the two classic modes of scientific thought, this enterprise has been vastly more inductive than deductive. We constructed, out of the rich body of data we gained through our interviews, a portrait of the sentencing process that would do justice to what we learned from some fifty individual voices and minds.

We did not expect to find the broad degree of consensus that is reflected in the judges' views, nor did we anticipate the extent to which those views are embedded in Anglo-American legal history. While not wishing to downplay clear and obvious cases of sentencing disparity, we think the finding of a consensus on the most general norms of harm, blameworthiness, and consequence provides hope for

30. Kenneth Mann, Stanton Wheeler, and Austin Sarat, "Sentencing the White Collar Offender," *American Criminal Law Review* 17, no. 4 (Spring 1980):479–500.

more just and effective sentencing. In order to move toward such systems, we will need better information and much more fine-tuning with regard to matters of weighting, combining, and anchoring the sentencing system. We will also need more jurisprudential thought on those many areas of sentencing where there is not a strong common-sense moral order that can be drawn upon by judges.

In the process of making these improvements and more generally in the process of developing rational systems of sentencing, there is much to be gained by learning, as we have tried to do in this study, from those who must deal with these matters on a daily basis. The study of judges, like that of the offenders they sentence, has an important place in the development of a workable criminal justice system.

More broadly, we have shown how individual judges, though coming from diverse backgrounds, training, and experience, are guided by a common sociolegal culture. We think this portrait, rather than the more familiar picture of a miscellany of individuals each heading off in his or her own ideological or emotional direction, more closely captures the social reality of sentencing in America. It also gives hope that the search for a more rational and consistent system of sentencing is not beyond reach.

Index

Actual conduct, centrality of, 17–18
Adversarial perspective: defense attorney and, 18, 49–52; in information process, 28–29
Age of defendant: blameworthiness and, 105; consequence of sentencing and, 151–52
Allocution, 52–53, 117–18
Altruism, as motive, 111
Ambiguity: economic loss and, 67–68; of indictments, 34–35
Anglo-American legal culture: common principles and, 13, 19–22; consequence in, 125; criminal responsibility and, 81, 82–87; factors in sentencing and, 166–67
Appellate review, 177
Aristotle, 82
Assault, 16
Assault with deadly weapon, 16, 61

Babylonian Talmud, 82
Bank employees, deterrence and, 139, 140
Bank robbery, 16, 62, 63, 65
Bankruptcy fraud, 15
Bank theft, 16
Beccaria, Cesare, 57–59, 125
Bentham, Jeremy, 125–28
Bishop, Joel Prentiss, 86
Blackstone, William, 59, 60n–61n
Blame: jurisprudence of, 175; shifting of, 116
Blameworthiness: assessment of, 93–123, 169, 176–77; common crime defendants and, 191; as common sentencing principle, 20–21, 22, 53, 81, 166; cooperation and, 118–20; criminal responsibility and, 23, 87–

92; degree of deliberateness and, 94–97; evidence for, from offense, 93–102; evidence for, from trial process, 112–20; guidelines and, 187n; life history and, 102–23; with multiple defendants, 97–102; prior record and, 88–92, 110–11, 184; translation problem and, 169–70; utilitarianism and, 172–73; weighting and, 169. *See also* Criminal responsibility
Blue-collar cases, and judicial empathy, 162–63
Bohanon, Paul James, 23
Bracton, Henry de 84
Bribery, 15, 174–75

Campaign contributions, illegal, 143
Case law, 24
Chiropractors, deterrence and, 144
Closing legal argument, 49
Commentaries on the Laws of England (Blackstone), 59
Common understanding about sentencing, 9–10, 166. *See also* Theory of sentencing
Community, and consequence, 152–56
Community service, 156, 158–60
Consequence of sentencing: assessment of, 124–65; as core legal norm, 125–33; for dependents, 152–56; for individual offender, 22, 124, 144–60; information on, in PSI, 179–80; judge's views of, 144–60; jurisprudence of, 175; measurement of, 169; prior record and, 184; as sentencing factor, 22, 53, 166; for society, 22, 124, 127n, 128n; translation problem and, 169–70

195

LIBRARY
MOUNT ... Y'S
COLLEGE
EMMITSBURG, MARYLAND

APR 22 1994